Finding Heart

Allow Yourself to Be You

Willow McIntosh

Dedication

To the unique adventure in you and the gifts it holds for all.

Acknowledgements

It is from the deepest part of my heart I would like to acknowledge:

Jeanne, my teacher and friend. Without your boundless patience and wisdom this book may have never materialised.

My wonderful daughter Ella-Louise. One of the greatest teachers I have had so far.

My dear family for the love, wisdom and the enormous fun that we have shared over the years. Thank you for not disowning me for the times I have sailed a little too close to the wind.

All the wonderful teachers and people I was fortunate enough to meet and work with along my travels; too numerous to list. Your kindness and commitment helped to make this material possible.

Contents

ABOUT THIS BOOK

Willow McIntosh was born in Sussex in the United Kingdom. Having studied psychology but not trained to be a psychologist or a psychotherapist why should you be reading this book? What does it have to offer and what is the material based on if not the conventional practices we are all used to hearing about?

This book has come about through a great deal of training and research over a period of about twenty years. It is the product of a non conventional path that was chosen as a result of following the guidance of the heart. An early fascination with expansion as a result of adventure began a quest for a particular type of knowledge. A playground of inquiry was born. Not only for personal experience but also for the facilitation of others to work through the blocks and feelings that hinder an attempt at discovering something new and something dear.

The chance to take this further came about with the choice to travel abroad at the age of twenty. A passion for outdoor sports had always provided an environment of adventure and further learning so training to become an instructor continued the passion for teaching. Helping others take the first steps into new learning and adventure coupled with the discipline of board riding in big seas meant a new vessel had emerged for spiritual understanding and the harnessing of energy and balance. From here a deeper journey into the heart was calling and the following year a pilgrimage began.

A seven year journey to every continent resulted in extensive work with a series of meditation teachers. Along the way specific techniques were personally practised and taught to process difficult feelings and thought patterns that often limited progress and the pursuit of truth. A personal discipline began to reveal that the natural feelings of contentment that we all have hidden within us are the route to what is authentic and true. This held the key to sharing the ability we all have to not only love ourselves but to reveal the adventure awaiting discovery within us all.

This book is a result of that journey and a continuing enquiry to this day into a passion for teaching and helping others find their way back to the calling inside. It is a commitment to love and truth. It is a gift to help realise the courage to do or become anything that is truly desired. The book is intended to talk to the heart as well as providing intellectual understanding. There are a series of steps found to be an effective way to re-learn the natural feelings of well being that reveal the truth and clear the blocks that contribute to non action. Rather than go into detail about what they are and how they work here it is more effective to allow the magic of the heart to take what it needs and open organically. Please help this process by being involved with the exercises and techniques in the book. By actively engaging we assist the heart and ourselves to get back to the place nature intended.

It is a wish that the content in this book is easy to follow, as effective as possible and as helpful as it can be. Please get in touch with any feedback or difficulties that may arise during the journey. Look for the contact details at the end of the book but feel free to make contact at any point. There is no need to have anything important to say and no need to make this journey alone.

"If you bring forth what is within you, what you bring forth will save you. If you do not bring forth what is within you, what you do not bring forth will destroy you."

— Gospel of Thomas

Introduction

If you have read the title to this book and began reading this page then I'm going to assume there is something you are longing to do or become. This book is going to discuss with you and show you how to do it with the patience and understanding of somebody who was exactly where you are right now. Whether this is a new business you would like to start, a particular lifestyle you would like to be living or a course of action you need to take.

The reason *why* you are not already doing it or *why* it keeps going wrong is what we are going to work through together. Consider that if we are trying to be like anyone else, trying to please anyone else or living our lives for anyone else we may not be giving ourselves much chance of living what we keep visualising and hoping for. Consider that if we are consistently giving our power away to old or misguided beliefs about the world and about ourselves the difficult feelings and blocks we are experiencing may also be the reason why we just can't seem to make anything happen.

By using tried and tested techniques we can undo these blockages which will help to ignite the fire and courage inside. Then we can begin getting in shape emotionally and psychologically to get us moving in the right direction. We will discover that the way we are thinking about ourselves, the world around us and other people in our lives is often what is hindering us. This will require Finding Heart to help us to think a little differently and try some new things and I know you are ready to do that now which is why you have this book in front of you.

As we read, our perception of what the words Finding Heart really mean to us will change and the personal meaning of this term can only be truly defined for ourselves. Finding Heart is not intellectual but an active process that helps us to create the right frame of mind and body to begin allowing ourselves to be who we really are. So rather than trying to find a particular result with a clear end as our minds would prefer, we are looking to relearn our authentic state of feeling good that in turn becomes our path. If we were to really embrace that right now we wouldn't need to read any further but in my experience revelations tend not to last long without practise. So once we begin practising the simple techniques in this book and nurture our relationship with Finding Heart we will begin to hear the guidance system to live our own adventure and feel the courage to follow it. But there is no magic cure or anyone that can do this for us because we must do the work ourselves. But *everyone* can do it.

The art of Finding Heart is a natural and reliable path to our own authenticity leading to the happiness and fulfilment we feel when we are doing something of our own creation. If you long to start a project, idea or journey that has been calling you, this book will help to open you to the part of yourself that is already in place to make it a reality.

This wonderful world we live in is a blank canvas awaiting our brush. It is here to support us in literally any type of work or endeavour we can conjure up. The only thing that ever stops us is ourselves. Learn to respond to and learn how to be guided by the heart. Witness for yourself that all this time your heart has been trying to show you that you are the perfect brush for the unique life endeavour you long for.

The world is set for adventures and modern society has everything we need. We don't need to complain anymore about what we don't have or how life could be different. We don't need to wait any longer for the right circumstances to emerge or for anything else. If you have a heart and a mind you are in the perfect state to begin and that state is now.

You can read this book in a couple of days and by the end of it you will have in your hands a practical way to keep the relationship with your hearts calling growing and alive. The more you include the techniques into your daily life you will see that one day at a time you are gradually starting to live the life and paint the picture that has always been there for you.

It is an art which is the wonderful and exciting part about it. Like any art it is a discipline that becomes a reassuring reference point with the reward of progress and learning. Just like any learning it comes with the pleasure of seeing ourselves grow and the best part about it is that the goal is living the adventure you have always dreamed of. Align with the most fulfilling thing in the world – yourself; see that everything you have needed to begin living the life or adventure you have always wanted is inside yourself.

Here is a little reassurance. If you are totally fed up, feeling unhappy, depressed and completely unmotivated then that is OK! I know how you are feeling because I have been there and if you keep reading and interacting with the content here soon you will be feeling much better and actually starting to do the very thing you wish you could. There will be some references to my life and experience to help bring context to the book but I have chosen not to use this space to tell my story because I do not want to detract from yours.

The fact we are feeling downright horrendous and hopeless is in fact really good news, it means our hearts are telling us we are not in the right room. The guidance system is working perfectly! We are simply not listening to our hearts, processing our feelings and being ourselves. We have got into the habit of living our lives for something else and forgotten who *we* are and what it is *we* need to be doing. It's simply a warning signal that we keep choosing the same street with the same hole in it and we keep blindly falling in day after day. Shall we stop a second, say hello to our hearts, apologise for not having been round to see them in such a time long and go and have a look together at that other street it keeps pointing at?

Before we begin:

1. Find a notepad & a pen
    (a new notepad you can
    dedicate to Finding Heart
    would be ideal) please use the notepad as you go
    through the book to write down thoughts, inspiration,
    progress and any questions you may have. The
    information you write down and the completion of the
    exercises will be the difference between Finding Heart
    and making progress or simply finding words and
    reading another book that you may soon forget.
    Interacting helps to process what we are learning,
    even in the smallest doing we are engaging and this
    will really help progress.

2. Stop for a moment to smile and relax. Please actually
    smile right now and allow your body to relax into your
    smile. From this moment forward choose to put down
    any sticks or any other weapons you like to carry
    around to beat yourself up with. If there is a tendency
    to administer yourself with mean self discipline to get
    a job done, please leave all that right here.

From this moment forwards into the book we take
compassion for ourselves, commitment and a light-
hearted sense of play. Remembering to relax into a smile
when our faces are all screwed up with worry and
judgement does wonders for Finding Heart ☺

I

Watering the Magic Beans

Are You Ready?

You have found this book because you are ready. You are ready to embark on your adventure and to do this you are going to need to find your heart. I know it's in your chest and you can feel it beating but can I just remind you it isn't there to just pump blood around; it's a whole lot more than that. This book has not been written specifically to help you find out what adventure you should take but to help you to know when the path you are choosing *feels* right so you stay on it. It is a living process and active awareness that we are going to learn together. It is the alignment with our own truth that will become the guide that is always there for us so we can stay on the daily path of our own adventure.

So how has that first paragraph made you feel? Is it sounding a bit 'spiritual' for you? In other words a little bit mystical and a bit out there? The whole living process and active awareness thing got your back up a bit? However you are feeling right now, take a chance and we can make this change as a team; you me and this book.

First let's check that a change of some sort needs to happen. If you are already on track in your life living your adventure and the path you know is right for you then I find it very unlikely you would have just paid for or been given this book. The fact we are ready to make a change is what leads us to find books like this one.

The change we are going to be looking at and learning to bring into our lives on a daily basis will bring us out of our heads and down into the world of our intuition. So the 'spiritual' is simply unchartered territory into the world of heart, trust me once you find your feet you will find it really good fun and ultimately fulfilling. Let's keep going...

By adventure I refer to the vision you have in your mind right now that you know you are going to achieve. You may not know how you are going to do it and that is great, we don't need to know how. But one way or another you can see yourself literally living through the day and doing the activities that mean you have got to where you want to be. This might be living in another country, it might be running the business you want or simply an undertaking that you have the self belief you can achieve.

It refers to anything we really want to do that involves us taking a leap of faith and being brave. Usually it is a decision that only we can make and one that is very dear to our hearts. The idea almost defines us and the longer we leave it before we realise this decision into action the more we sit in anguish and regret. This is the adventure of you, your adventure. You have had enough of the feeling of anguish and regret which is why you are now reading this.

So we are going to get used to the feeling of Finding Heart. We are going to begin to live it until it becomes second nature to us. It will become our map and the driving force that keeps us moving forwards on the right track. It will be what picks us up when we fall down, it will be the friend that welcomes us back no matter how long we have been away. It is the most genuine and authentic part of us and it is the most useful part when we have made the decision to start living our adventure.

A true feeling of value will come like a warm shower after working outside in the freezing rain when Finding Heart becomes our daily focus. Finding Heart will be what brings us to our adventure and in turn it will be our adventure that will bring a true feeling of value.

This process of Finding Heart will work for anything we undertake that has high stakes for us, so to put things in perspective we are going to call this our 'death bed' stakes. This sounds a little un-nerving and I know our aim is to keep things light-hearted and playful but that includes bringing reality and the wonderful importance of our adventure into the picture. So we need to do this now.

Death bed stakes are when we consider how we will feel about something in particular when we are lying on a bed and we know we are drawing on our last few breaths. It is accepting that something Is so important to us that when we imagine looking back over our life we feel utter relief we know we gave a particular adventure our very best. Knowing that there is a difference sometimes between doing our best and doing what has to be done. Shall we make a commitment together right now? Simply ignoring it because we can't face finding the courage to do it is only going to result in lying on our death bed wishing we had done something dear to our hearts. It might feel like it now but in reality we are not here for very long. By beginning this journey now we will help to ensure our deathbed is a place of satisfaction and gratitude. All we are asking of ourselves now is to simply put one foot in front of the other. So let's begin.

Our Commitment to our Adventure.

We are going to take a moment here to acknowledge the most important adventure, achievement or creative endeavour to *you* right now that you *know* you must undertake in this lifetime. As you read and practise with this book the good feelings Inside authentic to you will reveal whether or not the sentence you are about to write is genuinely coming from you or from somewhere or someone else. So it may be that we end up working with a slightly different version, exactly this or something entirely different. If you feel you just don't know what that might at the moment then I'm afraid I don't believe you. Remember you will only have yourself to answer to when you are old and drawing on your last few breaths. That old person is not going to listen to any excuses. Be honest and consider that there may be a fear of failure or a fear of success that is trying to hide it from you. At this stage we just need a simple sentence. No-one is going to read it and you can make changes later. An example is "The most important thing to me I will have done before I die is create an abundant life for myself and my family as an artist". Or "The most important thing to me I will be before I die is the owner of an eco spa retreat." To choose to be the best parent you can be for your children or to be happy are of course just as important but these things will come as natural by-products for you on a path with heart. We need something tangible and specific that you can actually begin to work with. Later in the book we are going to break it down into manageable steps so you can start to take action on it. If you have one in mind that makes you want to cry that's a great indication it is the one you should go with.

To find our sentence we are going to make friends with our heart and tune in. Please find somewhere to go and sit that is away from everyone else and a clear, calm space. Your bedroom may be ideal. Make the bed and briefly tidy the room if it needs it. The feeling in the room should be clear, peaceful and un-distracting.

- Sit somewhere comfortable with your back straight. If you prefer to sit cross legged stack some pillows on the bed to sit on so they support your posture.
- When you are comfortable pick up your notepad and write at the top 'Finding Heart Book'. Now make a heading underneath that says something along the lines of – "The most important thing to me I will be/will have done before I die is..."
- Put the notepad down.
- Put one hand onto the left side of your chest.
- As you take a deep breath in imagine the air is going all the way down to your feet.
- As you breathe out feel the air leaving your body is relaxing everything as it goes.
- Let go of any worry or expectation.
- Repeat the breathing several times until you feel relaxed and present.
- Now write down anything that is coming to you. It may be several things but try to get at least one thing down.

- Relax and don't worry if you aren't happy with the outcome of this. You will have plenty of time to work on it.

Before you get up to leave the room, whatever just happened here, take a moment to smile and feel proud of yourself that you are beginning the commitment to finding and following your heart ☺

On We Go!

When we think of the words Finding Heart it has two meanings; to 'find heart' in the sense that we find the heart or the courage to do something. In the second context it means to find the core, or the truth of ourselves. In my experience these two things have to be happening simultaneously for us to embark on our adventure. You have the courage for this adventure no matter where you are in your life right now and what your circumstances are. If there is something inside of you that you know is going to happen and you can see yourself doing it you will be on your way soon. You'll see.

Now just because our adventure is the most important work we can do and if we ignore it we may wither into regret does not mean we jump into almighty panic because we don't know how long we will live or we feel we are running out of time. Worry and panic are not in the Finding Heart tool box. They are states of mind that we will be learning to calm with love and acceptance which means they no longer have the means to engulf us.

In my experience of working with myself and others who are thinking about an adventure of some kind I find that what is actually in our hearts is often different to what our mind is expecting and seeing. The feeling we have in our heart when we visualise ourselves doing what we so wish to bring to fruition is then displayed in our minds as an idea of how that might look. This display can change slightly or it can stay as one image of how everything needs to go and if it doesn't start to go exactly as we are seeing it then we can stop in our tracks and announce to ourselves it isn't working. The actual journey of our adventure is exactly that, it is a journey. We have heard it a million times; success is a journey and not a destination. The rest of this quote says:

"Success is a journey, not a destination. The doing is often more important than the outcome."

If we think about it for long enough we can tell that life is happening to us in one giant moment. Everything from when we were born until now has been passing through the sensation of a moment that is still happening now. Yet when we dream of the future we often imagine it happening somewhere else. It might happen in another place such as another country but whatever is going to happen in the future is only going to pass through this giant now or moment. What I am trying to get at here is we only have to take our adventure one day at a time. The journey of success is going to happen one bit at a time and it's always going to do that. We're not going to suddenly arrive at a big destination with all that we imagined happening at once as if we were to walk through a particular door. So it is on a daily basis that we need to find heart and if we have not been able to do that for a part of the day all we need to do is focus on picking it up again.

The Heart of the Matter

(These points are reminders of key things for our hearts to take on board).

- ♥ Finding Heart is not intellectual but an active process that helps us to create the right frame of mind and body to begin allowing ourselves to be who we really are.
- ♥ As you read and practise with this book the good feelings inside authentic to you will reveal whether or not your chosen sentence is genuinely coming from you.
- ♥ There is no magic cure or anyone that can do this for us because we must do the work ourselves. But *everyone* can do it.
- ♥ The only thing that ever stops us is ourselves.
- ♥ We don't need to wait any longer for the right circumstances to emerge or for anything else.
- ♥ We only have to take our adventure one day at a time.
- ♥ It is the alignment with our own truth that will become the guide that is always there for us.
- ♥ By beginning this journey now we will help to ensure our deathbed is a place of satisfaction and gratitude.
- ♥ Relax and smile! Have another go right now.
- ♥ Take a moment to add any observations or resistance you are feeling into your notebook. These reactions, feeling and insights are our guidance system talking to us. ☺

You Have Done This Before...

I know you can get back on your path to Finding Heart and living your adventure because you are a human being. You were designed for it! You already have all the tools you need. You have heart, you have passion, you have vision, so do I and this is all we need to embark on this journey together.

I understand if everything right now is just horrendous, I really understand. I assure you I have been there in the pits of despair feeling as though nothing in life is working and I seem to be incapable of doing anything of value. I have had awful periods of my life in depression bought on because I would not accept who I was and what it was I needed to do. It is from this place that I learned to find heart using the techniques in this book and I started to live my truth again. It is possible; you know that because *you* have done it before as well. So in these next couple of sections we are going to recall our own innate ability of Finding Heart. Remember this process is all about *allowing* rather than learning something new.

I'm going to invite you to think back to a time in your life when you felt really happy. It may have been a part of your childhood or perhaps when you first left home or maybe when you were away in another country. Think back to a bright part of your life when you felt as though life was flowing, when everything seemed to make sense and you felt content.

Whatever, wherever and whenever that was you were living in alignment with your heart and that is why it felt so right. It doesn't matter if it feels like our happiness was out of our hands back then because of other people or circumstances around us. We are simply looking to recall the passion again now so our body can remember it. If we allow it this feeling *is* available to us again and it will help to reignite the desire to take our adventure into our own hands. Even if it is going against the grain of everyone else but *with* the grain of our own feelings, we shall begin to find heart again. What's exciting is this part of ourselves never actually went away and with the time that has passed in between then and now it brings with it new wisdom, new experience and a new you.

The Feeling of Flow.

Take a chance and relive a period of happiness by describing it and answering the questions below in your notepad. Once again if you believe you have never felt happy before I'm afraid I don't believe you, try not to over think it and *allow* yourself to recall a period of your life when everything seemed to flow well for you. It needs to be more than an afternoon, it can be short but it needs to be a stretch of time. There will be insight for you in this that will help guide you into creating a new version of this flow that is well suited to you now. You know the period of your life I am referring to, go on you can do it. Try to relive the feelings, the sounds and even the smells.

- What was so fulfilling and joyful about it?
- What is it about that time that felt so right?
- What is it that was allowing you to blossom and grow?
- What do you think it is about this time that you valued the most?
- Do you feel you could allow yourself to feel like that again now? (If your answer right now is 'No', that is fine. Just for now try to recall the feeling as best as you can).
- Close your eyes, smile and allow yourself to return to that time again now if you can.
- When you are ready open your eyes and gently come back into the room.

The Leap of Faith.

Perhaps that last exercise bought some sadness aswell, if it did that's ok. All your feelings are welcome, valid and part of the process. Let's keep going...

The very fact that you are here right now means that you have the tools and abilities to survive and to take risks. This may sound obvious but it's easy to forget the instances when we have been brave in the past. By recalling these as well we will remember that we can trust ourselves and we will be OK when things get tricky. So we are going to think carefully to find specific examples.

Begin to list the times in your notebook that you felt pride for yourself for doing what needed to be done in the moment. For instance when you tried something new or did something that took all of your courage. Again we don't need to over think it, instead simply begin writing down anything that comes to mind. Was there anything potentially risky you did as a child or as a young adult? Maybe you had to rescue an animal or a friend or maybe there was an adventure sport you tried. Perhaps it was a job interview for a position that at the time seemed beyond you.

Take the time and you will find them. With these examples try to remember the feeling of the fear before hand and the experience of being OK the other side. These memories will trigger the feeling of how we found the heart before and by recalling them we are reminding ourselves we *do* have courage inside us, we *have* got things done in the past so we *can* do it again.

Now write down what you had to do to make these things happen.

- What might you have had to temporarily given up to allow yourself this experience? (Perhaps a voice or belief you weren't good or strong enough?)
- How did you go about helping yourself to do it or get there before? (Perhaps something you said to yourself? Or was there a particular feeling in your body that helped you finally find the courage to do it?)

Did you notice that finding the courage often means stepping out of our comfort zone? Taking a leap of faith happens when our mind can only take us 80% of the way, the remaining step into the unknown always takes heart. This is the plant of heart we are looking to carefully uncover and bring back out into the sunlight again now. The more our little plant is acknowledged as our personal source of strength, guidance and deep contentment the bigger and stronger it becomes. Take a moment to acknowledge and celebrate this strength and courage you have inside. We are going to take it with us.

So we have just recreated from our memory two very important experiences. One is the feeling of flow and deep contentment of living in line with our heart and the other is finding the courage to take a leap of faith. Right here is evidence of previous experience of two principles of Finding Heart that we have as a natural ability; to live our truth and to find the courage needed to act in line with it.

I think this is cause for a little celebration, don't you? Take a deep breath in, throw your arms in the air and with a big grin say 'YES! I am Finding Heart' ☺

Finding Heart Again Now

"Leap and the net will appear" — John Burroughs.

When we are young adults we need to start living our own lives, not our parent's and this process is necessary to develop our independence. It's our first experience of finding the courage and the heart to take a leap of faith and leave the house by ourselves. It is a chance to go and live out our ideas according to our desires, interests and passion. Something drives us that may be nowhere on the radar of our parent's ideas for us but we take action anyway.

So what leads to this important breakthrough that gets us out there and following our hearts?

- Consider there is a persistent feeling that calls us to start going our own way.
- We begin looking for the opportunities available to us.

- We try something new, get a taste for it and perhaps speak to someone who is doing what we want to do. This all leads to the powerful experience that we do have the courage to try new things for ourselves in the world outside of our family home.

This is an example in our lives when we put the right feeling and courage together to make something happen. Perhaps as a young adult we made a few mistakes that we have since learned from but we committed ourselves according to how we felt at the time. Did we survive those mistakes? Were many of them in fact useful for us to learn about the world and about ourselves? Of course! This is what we can begin to do again now. We don't have to stop paying the rent or the mortgage until we make our idea a reality or leave our job and never come back. But we can commit to making our lives line up with the good feeling in our heart.

Perhaps more may be at stake to live out our dreams now because we have less time, more responsibility and life circumstances are different. Maybe life seems so much harder now than when we were younger. Perhaps the stakes seem higher if it goes wrong. But don't forget that now we have experience and some wisdom to take with us whilst the concept is still exactly the same.

So what is the concept that leads us to live in alignment with our truth?

It is the good sensation in the core of our body that feels in alignment with our thinking, values and wish we have for our growth. We also believe it can happen. This is what we are going to learn to do again now with the techniques and exercises in this book. Remember all we are doing is uncovering an ability we already have.

The belief we can have be or do something is essential. If we don't *believe* we can then we need to carefully contemplate if the plan we have is genuine inspiration coming from ourselves.

Begin to trust that we know what it is *we* need to do. Trust that we do know the feelings in our gut that will lead to the results we are looking for; it is the feeling that makes sense to us. We aren't looking for thunderbolts from heaven necessarily or great flashes of light for confirmation. It is the personal feeling we have when something feels right to us. That is what we are looking for.

Sometimes we prefer to ignore what feels right because it's scary but when we choose to commit to our journey it will unfold one day and one heartfelt decision at a time. We are not going to be transported to an end result all of a sudden, if we tried to make that happen we would probably fall over.

Remember that life won't throw anything at us that we can't handle. We have an innate ability to bring ourselves through even the most difficult life circumstances. We know this because we have done it before. It's about letting go and simply getting on with what we know is right for us. Remember that older you is waiting!

Life has a way of yielding and processing mistakes so we don't need to worry ourselves to a standstill. We can't stop things going wrong by mistake, hurting loved ones by mistake or perhaps making mistakes when we are working. We always have a choice to take responsibility, apologise, make it right and learn.

Our hearts guide us to evolve in a way that is most suited to who we are as individuals and when we are in alignment with our hearts we are taken care of as if by magic. This has been my experience and I know if you think back to your examples it will be the same for you. When we are in alignment with who we are we emanate good feeling and that is what comes back. Life wants it; our job is to allow it.

Finding Heart is often about letting go, letting go into the awareness that we cannot control life. In our minds we do our best to try to control it but it is our hearts that have the wisdom to respond and guide us along the rocky path we must all take. The decisions we make shape us and we can choose to evolve into the life that feels right for us or not, it is up to us and us alone.

So from these examples and experiences we can explore how our own heart unfolds. If you are sitting there with your nose in the air and reading this saying to yourself, "No I have never done anything remotely similar to what he is talking about. I have never done anything that required courage and to trust the feelings in my body into a leap of faith that became something amazing". Well this was exactly what you did when you learned to walk and you can apply exactly the same concept again now. If you are insistent you have never felt happy and with the flow of your natural heartfelt contentment and joy remember this is exactly the state we were born with and what we carried into our childhood. It is always there for us, it's just waiting for us to *allow* it again.

We may be unique and our paths are ours alone but the process of Finding Heart is a universal one and by working with these experiences it becomes a formula we can learn that will soon become as bespoke as we are. If the adventure we have in mind is our own version and one we believe in, we will achieve it. Right there is everything we need.

So please honour and respect what you have written in the commitment exercise, whatever that may be. The trick is to be as honest as you can with how you are feeling about it as you read on. If you are feeling some comparison to someone else's adventure let that fall away. There is no better or more advanced, only different angles of perception. Each flavour of perception, no matter who it is coming through, is just as awesome and powerful as the next. We are all on a journey that aligns with our own values and our own wishes for our growth. It cannot be better or worse than someone else's and how it may look to someone else is none of our business. It doesn't matter if that journey is setting up a business making woollen rabbits for children or finding the heart to move to a new place and begin a new life. It holds just as much magic and power in it as anyone else's journey and don't let anyone make you think differently.

The Heart of the Matter

- ♥ You can get back on your path to Finding Heart and living your adventure because you are a human being. You were designed for it! You already have all the tools you need.
- ♥ What's exciting is this part of ourselves never actually went away and with the time that has passed in between then and now it brings with it new wisdom, new experience and a new you.
- ♥ The very fact that you are here right now means that you have the tools and abilities to survive and to take risks.
- ♥ Taking a leap of faith happens when our mind can only take us 80% of the way; the remaining step into the unknown always takes heart.
- ♥ We are looking for the good sensation in the core of our body that feels in alignment with our thinking, values and wish we have for our growth. We must also believe it can happen.
- ♥ The belief we can have be or do something is essential. If we don't *believe* we can then we need to carefully contemplate if the plan we have is genuine inspiration coming from ourselves.
- ♥ It is the personal feeling we have when something feels right to us. That is what we are looking for.
- ♥ Keep those times in your life you have been courageous and acted out of instinct and a personal source of courage at the forefront of your mind.
- ♥ Our hearts want us to evolve in a way that is most suited to who we are as individuals.
- ♥ Take a moment to add any observations or resistance you are feeling into your notebook

So Why Did We Feel So Happy Before?

"When the heart speaks, the mind finds it indecent to object."
Milan Kundera

Why does everything seem to work so well during those happy periods in our lives? An elusive yet vital part of Finding Heart is living in line with our values. Our values are our deep core beliefs. We often live outside of our values and this can be one of the main contributing factors to unhappiness. We are going to need to get back into synchronicity with them by getting intimate with our needs and respecting ourselves in a deeper sense than perhaps we are used to. Our values can be a little tricky to identify at first but they are a very important part of the concept we have just been looking at and they need further examination.

Why are our values so important to Finding Heart? It's easier to begin by talking about what happens if we are *not* living in alignment with our values. For instance if one of our values or deep core beliefs is truthfulness and we take a sales job that requires us to pitch a story about a product we don't believe in, this means we will have to lie and this is going to cause problems. If we rent a room out in our apartment to a man who is very messy and disorganised and we value cleanliness and order in our living environment we are not going to last long as flat mates. This would be a key conversation we would have during the interview about living habits. So an effective way to uncover our values is by asking the question in any situation "What is most important to me about this?"

But remember our values are not revealed to us by thinking alone and many of what we think are *our* core beliefs are being influenced by someone or something else. A good example is money, if we are told over and over that being wealthy is for bad people this could begin to feel like that is our belief or value. But in fact we have taken this on from somewhere else and it is not necessarily what we believe. So when we are asking the question "What is most important to me about this?" we must await a particular feeling!

When one of our values emerges on a particular topic or experience it is when it *feels* right. The penny drops and it feels like a strong place with good foundation. We get a sense of connection, belonging, self confidence and we can feel it is ours. We are going within and then aligning to what is *genuinely true* to us and so the resulting effect is an experience of strength through personal veracity. This is what was happening in the time in our lives when we were most happy that we identified previously.

The identification of our values will take practise but I'm sure you can see now why learning to do it is so important. The particular adventure we have in mind that we want to pursue after reading this or while we are reading this *must* be in alignment with *our* values. Otherwise we are heading for trouble.

"I never went into business just to make money - but I found that if I have fun, the money will come. I often ask myself, is my work fun and does it make me happy? I believe that the answer to that is more important than fame or fortune".

-Richard Branson

This is a great example of why many businesses fail. According to the Small Business Administration, about two-thirds fail within the first two years. About 56 per cent of businesses fail at the five-year mark. They go on to speculate reasons for this, 'Most businesses do not make a profit during their first years and owners may not have the passion or persistence to keep running the business efficiently and learn from their mistakes'.

Any venture we undertake means we have to think carefully that it is in alignment with *our* values, whether it is a move to another country, a relationship or a business. When Richard Branson asks himself the question "Is my work fun and does it make me happy?" what he is really asking himself is "Is this in alignment with *my* values?"

It is no use going into a venture convinced it is right for us because our parents think it is. Or undertaking something for the benefit of someone else, if we really want to help others we must first begin with true compassion for ourselves by taking our core beliefs very seriously. Then we will be of much more use to everyone around us. Being around anyone who is very clear on their values in a particular situation, workplace or even at home is very refreshing. They can almost seem quite cold in their approach sometimes which one would except to be repelling, but you will find that anyone who is very clear about how they feel is very encouraging to be with. Think of key figures like Ghandi, Mother Theresa or Nelson Mandela. They are so attuned with their values thousands of people will flock to follow them.

Be the Ghandi of your values and get very clear on everything and anything that is confronting you. Often when someone trips us over with a comment or a remark it is because they are reflecting back to us something we are not clear on in our selves. If someone comments on something we are doing and it makes us feel angry and upset then what do *we* really think about what we are doing? If we are firmly in alignment with our values in whatever venture it may be it shouldn't matter to us what someone else says about it. (Although in the early stages whilst we are getting all this into place it is best we *don't* go around testing this out. This will become clearer in the section 'Who do we talk to about our adventure?')

If we are thrown off balance by someone else then it may be that we are running a judgement on our own value that is in effect *shadowing* our true value. We may well be in alignment with our own values but the comment from someone else has triggered a false belief we have about it. Here is an example, perhaps we have taken a new job and a close friend makes fun of it in some way but it really affects us and we feel quite upset. We may get upset because we have a judgement about our own value running that indicates they are right and the job is a bad choice. This is where we need to begin asking the question "What is most important to me about this job?" We then wait for the feeling we recognise that confirms it is truly of value to us. If we discover that what we genuinely feel is in agreement with our friend and the job is no good for us then the whole interaction has been useful and we have discovered a truth that needed addressing.

If we discover that in fact the job holds an opportunity for us that is very much in alignment with something we value very much then we have uncovered a value that seemed to be hidden to us or one we were not respecting before. This chance to bring it into the forefront will reveal the real reason we took the job in the first place and subsequently we don't need to worry what other people think about it.

Our values are very much part of our guidance system but they are not something we can find tattooed to the soles of our feet unfortunately. Our values are simply something we are already living by or we are in conflict with them. We have values concerning each aspect of our lives and our view of the world. We have values about work, religion, sex, the life we choose to live etc etc.

Being clear on them is important but living outside of our values is not as obvious as putting our hand in fire. We could have been living outside of our values for ages, we know something is not right but we can live with the discomfort. This is not living in alignment with our truth so we must ensure that whatever we are considering for ourselves now *is* in alignment with our values.

This doesn't necessarily mean that we need to recreate the exact circumstances of the time in our lives when we felt truly happy and content. To try to replicate a period of happiness to the letter may not be taking into consideration how we are feeling now because along the way our needs may have changed. We can't live in the past because our hearts are operating in the now.

For instance some of my values are adventure, independence and freedom. When I was travelling abroad it didn't matter to me where I lived and this period of my life was one of the best for me. I still the love the adventure of travel but I need a base to come back to now. So if I was to uproot with a pack on my back and never look back like I used to it wouldn't be taking my current need of a base into consideration. I was happy during that period of my life because it was in alignment with my values but now I must respect the fact that I value stability as I have got older.

When we have a value conflict going on it can appear that we are fighting ourselves and nothing seems to be moving forwards. All the work in the world can appear futile when there is a value conflict in there. So it's important that we feel into what our values are and whether the venture we are considering is in alignment with them.

I can't recommend exploring this enough. Please open a new section in your notepad and title it 'My Values' and begin to list what you value the most about as many aspects of life as you can think of. For example you could write the sentence 'What is most important to me about..? Then begin to feel for what you value most about that experience of life. It's all about getting really clear on what is most important to *you*. Now we are opening to the world of heart we are getting more intimate with our feelings and the guidance they are to us. Now the idea of values is on our radar they will begin to emerge. Break down the statement you made in the commitment exercise as your values emerge to you and it will soon become clear if it needs adjusting or working on. The ability it has to weather the storms it will meet along the path will be in direct correlation to how aligned it is to your values.

Take a breather and let all that settle in for a moment. There is no rush here, allow yourself to process this in your own time.

Take a deep breath in.... And when breathing out let everything fall down through your body and into the ground. Gather yourself in this moment, aaaah. You are doing great... Ok... On we go!

Finding Heart in Fish

"Nothing great was ever achieved without enthusiasm."
Ralph Waldo Emerson

Before we move on I would like to include a lovely example of Finding Heart in alignment with values that we may see every day but perhaps don't stop to acknowledge. On my walk home this evening I decided to take a different route. I felt inspired to walk into a particular street that has a building at the end that interests me. Usually I can only go as far as the building but then I have to walk back up the same street because it has a 'dead end'. Many years before I had walked down this street to see what was going on in this building only to find a dance class called 'The 5 Rhythms.' I happened to be in my suit at the time but the good sensation in my body that led me down the street also led me to say yes when the teacher invited me to take part. I had an incredible experience of release and joy in the class that meant I would go on to join the group and have many experiences of joy and alignment; a great example of finding the heart to go where the good feeling takes us.

On this occasion of visiting the street I discovered a little muse that meant I could find a new way through to my road and this led me to notice a new fish restaurant. It looked lovely, very cute and cosy with just twenty covers or so. It was painted on the outside in a matt charcoal with cream lettering and inside it was lit in a warm glow. It had lovely wooden floors and distressed white furniture, it looked inviting. Through the window I could see written on the blackboard that it was opening on 15th January which was only two days ago at the time. On the ledge of the floor to ceiling window by my feet were the menus in little wooden frames with tiny writing. I had to crouch down to read them and so the owner came out to greet me. 'They're a bit small.' I said smiling. 'I know' he replied beaming. 'I came out to greet you because I couldn't leave you like that trying to read them'. He went on to explain that he was going to get bigger ones for the window but had put some table menus there for the time being. I could sense in him the enthusiasm and brightness of a person who had created a new life in line with his values.

As I got talking to him, this man described the journey and trials he had faced in converting the restaurant from a fish mongers. He proudly told me about his decisions to serve particular dishes here, the coffee he had chosen and how he had painstakingly designed the restaurant to achieve what he had envisioned. We chatted for a while and I got a real sense of what he had been through to get his new restaurant open. The time and money he had invested and the chance it would fail in the current economic time. But he had gone for it and from his energy I could tell it was truly his choice from his heart and he would find the strength and innovation to make it a success. He had built the stage to serve his food to the world and live his dream. Can you imagine what he might have learned and experienced along the way? The doing is more important than the outcome and now that he has finally opened it *the journey continues*. He found the heart to create something in alignment with what he values most and that is what will lead him on.

Our lives have been an adventure so far, not all of us survive to get to our age. Many of us don't make it. We make the wrong decisions, fall ill or take our own lives. But you and I have made it this far. We should be amazed at the courage we were born with and if we are disappointed that so far we have not lived life as a daring adventure then now is the time to begin. As the Chinese proverb says, "The best time to plant a tree is twenty years ago or now!"

The Heart of the Matter

- We often live outside of our values and this can be one of the main contributing factors to unhappiness.
- When one of our values emerges on a particular topic or experience it is when it *feels* right. The penny drops and it feels like a strong place with good foundation.
- The particular adventure we have in mind that we want to pursue after reading this or while we are reading this *must* be in alignment with *our* values
- If we really want to help others we must first begin with true compassion for ourselves by taking our core beliefs very seriously.
- Be the Ghandi of your values and get very clear on everything and anything that is confronting you.
- To try to replicate a period of happiness to the letter may not be taking into consideration how we are feeling now because along the way our needs may have changed.
- It's all about getting really clear on what is most important to *you*.
- The best time to plant a tree is twenty years ago or now!
- Take a moment to add any observations or resistance you are feeling into your notebook ☺

Our Adventure and the Mind.

"My heart knows what my mind only thinks it knows."
Noah Benshea

Have you ever stopped to notice the chatter your mind is constantly producing? The constant flow of thought we experience throughout the day that often seems completely unrelated to anything we are actually doing. When we start to think about this objectively we are engaging the awareness we all have which allows us to *observe* our own thoughts rather than *react* to them. So to help us make progress on our journey we are going to learn how to parent the mind.

In my experience we often create imaginary brick walls for ourselves because we are giving our mind authority over us. Our minds are incredible but they are fickle. They can be like a child with a toy when it comes to things we hold dearly in our hearts. Without meaning to our mind can throw something important over its shoulder and if we don't learn to catch it again it will hinder progress. Especially since the thought of our vision or adventure is often daunting for all sorts of reasons.

Our minds cannot help telling us what it thinks is best for us or painting us a picture of what our adventure is going to look like in the future. It can invent all sorts of possible eventualities, circumstances and likely outcomes which are based in fear or unfounded imagination. We are meaning making machines. By this I mean we cannot help but make everything that we witness inside or outside of ourselves mean something, we don't have to take all the meanings we make on board. If we were to act on or believe everything that our minds produce we would end up going mad. Our minds are not our guidance system and ninety percent of the daily chatter is not coming from a higher awareness. There's nothing wrong with that, but it is just chatter. So the process of Finding Heart must include the practise of dropping us down and out of our heads into our bodies so we can get to feel our inspiration and intuition. This grounds us so we are not constantly blown around by the chatter.

There will be more on this in the section 'Thoughts & Voices' along with a series of exercises to help us. At this stage we just need to become aware of our minds activity and habits and to recognise the ways in which our thoughts can sabotage progress and keep us stuck from making any progress at all. We must learn to recognise our minds as a tool and not our master. If we let our minds run riot and take the reins we are at the mercy of a powerful processing device that has the influence to cripple us into non action based on something it has completely made up.

There is an unnerving place we all allow ourselves to go when we just seem to stop in mid flow and begin to question everything. We let our minds go, literally, like a wild horse that just bolts and kicks across a field with no agenda or purpose apart from letting off steam. The problem is when our minds worry us like this we tend to believe everything it produces. We don't need to believe everything our mind thinks.

So when we allow our minds to think back to experiences we have had in the past that have made us unhappy we might associate them with our current reality. We might begin to create all sorts of reasons in our mind why we are not good enough or not deserving of our adventure. To not be good enough for our own adventure is impossible! It is impossible not to be good enough to manifest our own authentic path because it is our divine right. *Only* we have what it needs to make it manifest.

We may need help along the way but no-one else has our vision; we are the architect. Even if we are looking to recreate something that has been done before, our vision of it is unique only to us. If the adventure is truly authentic to us and honestly coming from our hearts then we have everything we need to make it happen. It would be like telling a healthy dog with four legs it isn't good enough to run. It has everything it needs to run, to run where the dog instinctively feels it wants to run. 'Not being good enough' is one of our insane thought patterns that we must learn to quiet if we are going to Find Heart and become the adventure.

I don't mean to unnerve you by saying we can't trust our minds. Our thoughts can be triggered in many ways, sometimes in a way that is very much our making. That is then sincere, that is intelligent and to be taken seriously. I am not disputing that in any way. But consider this scenario...

You are walking home one afternoon and you pass an advert on a wall. It is a picture of a person looking very chic in a new outfit. Perhaps it is a perfume or after-shave advert and the person in the picture looks really happy. The mind then does something like this – "Ooh that person looks very happy in that cool outfit; I bet they are really happy. I wonder what they are doing right now. I bet they have an amazing job the perfect partner and loads of money. I bet they are living in the perfect house. They are so lucky, I wish I had all that, I bet I never get any of that. I'd never look that good in that outfit..."

Ever had this sort of thing run through your head? This is the kind of madness I am referring to. It is simply the mind off on an unchecked jaunt. It is not to be taken seriously or believed in. It is random thought association triggered from a picture on a wall and it's perfectly normal for our mind to be doing it. But the mind is fickle, it could end up anywhere. If you let it keep going it would have ended up with an unhappy outcome. *"I bet I never get any if that, I would never look good in that outfit!"* The mind doesn't mean to upset us, it is just processing.

Taking the chatter seriously is a big contributing factor to why we are not living our adventure or living in flow with our truth. We are often getting intuition and calling from our hearts, we are often getting indication about what is important to us via our feelings. We have dreams and visions of the lives we know are best suited to us but we get a lot more noise and general static from our minds on a day to day basis.

The example of the model in the picture illustrates how the mind can inadvertently cause us discomfort *if* we allow it. When we focus on a thought and give it meaning it will create feeling in us. In the case of the model we might generate a feeling of low self esteem. This feeling now feels real to us and all of a sudden it affects our mood and our actions triggered from a picture that has no base in reality whatsoever.

If it can happen as easily as that then what stories are we making up about a course of action that will lead us to a life that we know will make us truly happy? Unfortunately our minds inherently associate in negativity as much they do in positivity and often it will seem as though there is no particular reason for one or the other. So for our purpose of getting back in line with what our hearts desire for us we have no choice but to choose which thoughts we entertain about our adventure and about ourselves.

For the next coming day or so run an experiment with your mind. See how many times you can pull yourself out of a negative thought pattern. In other words see how many times you can catch your mind and bring yourself back to the present moment. You can do this by bringing your attention back to one of your senses such as the feeling of your breathing, the sounds you can hear or the feeling of your feet on the ground. Learn to notice when the mind starts running a set of thoughts that feel negative or are simply *not true*. Don't forget to smile, smiling is very important if the thought process was a negative one. Think of how a parent knowingly smiles without judgement when their child suddenly goes bananas for no apparent reason.

As you practise you will get an insight into what is authentic useful information and noise. We can choose what we believe and take seriously and with this exercise we are simply introducing some awareness. We cannot stop our minds from generating thought. But we can stop negative thought processes when they arise. From working with the idea that much of the incessant chatter in our minds is responsible for building the walls that stop us from making constructive progress, we can begin to see that the walls were never there in the first place. See what you notice and take this awareness of the mind with you as we go into the next section. If you find much of the chatter is derogatory and putting you down, what affect do you think this might be having on progress?

If Only I was Different I'd be Happy?!

Just as we can make up stories about the world around us we have a tendency to do exactly the same about ourselves. There are parts of our personalities and character that we sometimes label as bad or broken. In some cases for many years or even most of our lives, but it is often in our darkest recesses our gifts can be residing. If we could make parts of our character we don't like disappear by being judgemental we would have done it by now. These parts of ourselves are part of who we are and whilst it can seem they are intensely annoying and only a hindrance we must learn to accept and welcome all our various facets as part of the team.

When we are *allowing ourselves* to understand and accept who we are we involve and *respect* all aspects of ourselves. So getting back in line with the flow of good heartfelt contentment is also dependent on holding ourselves to account about the opinions and judgments we make about ourselves. Otherwise we are simply building more imaginary walls to block the flow. We do this by acknowledging and working with the positive that each aspect brings to the table.

If we happen to be highly sensitive for example this has its benefits and gifts. It doesn't mean we have an excuse not to live our lives fully or decide we aren't good enough to get involved with things. Consider a part of your own personality that you are aware of that seems to make you really unhappy. If you had to find a positive to it, what would that be? (We will look at this more closely in the exercise at the end of this section).

Let take the example of being highly sensitive. To begin with we will look at the apparent problem of having a sensitive central nervous system and what can be termed a 'highly sensitive person'. This might make sense to you and resonate or it may not. It means there is a tendency to feel anything that passes near or through the body very acutely. So when something goes wrong or something happens that means overload and anxiety; the thoughts and feelings associated can be very strong and bring us to a standstill. If we are easily affected by the outside world it might mean we are distracted from what we are doing, our own values and our goals.

But when we accept this is a part of who we are we will begin to see how important it is for our chosen adventure. Nothing is there by mistake. With acceptance we can also learn how to respect a particular part of our design by choosing the types of scenarios we subject ourselves to. If we are highly reactive then we can't walk around like an open book trying to connect with everyone and anyone in all types of environments. We would go mad and into over load very quickly with all sorts of reactions and feelings.

Being highly sensitive means a person can be very intuitive and can read people well. It also means that there can be a deep intimacy of feelings and experience and an acute creativity that can be harnessed. The gift that is residing here suddenly becomes an important tool for our journey when we allow and accept it.

I invite you to think differently about the parts of your character or design that you wish were different. The more we can accept ourselves the more we will be able to work *with* ourselves when we are following our dreams and walking our adventure. Rather than label parts of our personalities as broken let's get clear about what these parts actually are and what advantages they bring to the table. The last thing we want to do is try to hide parts of our personality and character wishing they weren't there.

Perhaps we wish they weren't there sometimes because of what we *think* other people are thinking about them. Are we comparing ourselves to others? Are we noticing we are different and deciding that the part of us that is different is wrong? This is a negative thought process to look out for and not one to entertain. If we feel negatively about a part of our personality other people are likely to see it as negative which only perpetuates the problem. This part of Finding Heart is about learning to lovingly accepting the heart of who we are. If we are genuinely looking to walk the adventure of who we are and follow our individual path we are going to have to get very honest about who we are.

It does worry me when I come across people in meditation centres and personal development trainings, seminars and workshops who are 'not happy with you they are'. They have decided they have come out the factory broken and once they have fixed all the parts of themselves they feel are wrong they will then start living their lives. Isn't it the war we are waging on ourselves that causes so much pain and disharmony inside? If we can learn to understand all the parts of ourselves on an intimate level and learn to live according to our needs we will find that all the parts of our personalities have a purpose and they serve us.

If you can relate to this, notice any tension in your body right now, take a deep breath, and let go of that gripping feeling you may have inside for a moment. We are working together to discuss and learn effective ways to learn to be with all of who we are. Our aim is to feel great about keeping ourselves in line with our own path and that path includes every facet of our character.

Dark places of rejection and abandonment are often created because someone else could not handle a part of us or a way in which we behave. This could be because they can't accept it in themselves or they don't have the emotional flexibility to accept and work with this part of us. Our own decision that we are wrong or broken can be made when we are very young, it becomes our shadow; parts of us we carry about on our backs as baggage that we wish we could put down. We have buttons that are easily pushed and we have reactions that make us feel ashamed, sad and angry.

Finding Heart is about getting clear on how *we* genuinely feel about a particular part of our behaviour or character. In fact we will often attract people into our lives that do push our buttons, our partners, friends and siblings can all be really good at finding the parts of us we find it so hard to accept. They are reflecting back to us parts of ourselves we simply need to make friends with, we can shine a light onto parts of ourselves we have been repressing for years. We can also be compassionate with ourselves that there are parts of our personalities that we are sensitive to, parts that we are learning to incorporate into our experience in a healthy way by noting the positive and the purpose they serve.

Learning to process painful feelings and reactions and stop judgemental thoughts from running out of control is essential to leading a happy life. If we let our minds run wild and make up all sorts of fear based meanings about ourselves it will stop us from taking healthy action. The overwhelming feelings that came from these thoughts busy and cloud our systems to such an extent we have no way of hearing what we want or need. We can't do this and live our lives aligned with who we truly are. In the section on 'Thought and Voices' we will learn techniques that will help us to process ourselves and give us tools we can use to break the habit of keeping ourselves stuck.

So next time you decide a part of yourself is broken consider the positive side to it you may well be hiding from. Look into the darkness and see the gift that is waiting to express itself and help you. We become so addicted to running negativity through our engineering and then we wonder why things aren't working properly. We are going to make a conscious shift into positivity soon when we come to the section called 'The Power of Feeling Good' but for now take with you this key element to Finding Heart, honouring the essence of who we are. This means all our facets; we blossom when we *allow* and accept ourselves. When we stop resisting and shift to persisting from a place of love our actions become aligned with who we really are.

Finding the Positive in a Personality "Flaw"

1. Please turn to your notebook and be as honest as you can here.
2. Write down a part of your personality that you struggle with and wish was different or write down a part of your behaviour that seems to make you unhappy and you wish was different.
3. What does a negative view of this part of your personality afford you? In other words what excuses do you make up because of this part of yourself?
4. Now pretend you could take away this part of your personality. Who would you be? What would your life become?
5. Just for the purpose of this exercise find a positive side to this part of your personality. It can be anything at all, even the smallest thing will do.
6. What do *you really feel* about this part of your personality yourself? Not what other people think of it.
7. If there was a gift for you in this part of this personality what could that be? There is one there! You don't need to over think it.
8. What purpose do you think this part of your personality will serve in getting you closer to what you wrote in the commitment exercise?
9. Compare this to what you wrote in number 4 of this exercise. Would you prefer what you wrote in the commitment exercise? Is there a possibility this part of your personality is necessary for where you are going?

Writing down this information urges us to investigate parts of ourselves we think are broken. It will help us to become aware of the different parts of them for ourselves and help us to see they have their place. Even if they do appear to have a negative aspect, learn to develop the positive side and begin to notice the affect it has on you and the people around you.

Now please put everything down and stand up. Shake your arms, legs and head whilst dancing around in a little circle. Don't forget to open your mouth, stick your tongue out and let it wiggle freely from side to side whilst making a silly noise. When you have finished a couple of laps around the room go and stand in front of a mirror and relax. Feel your feet on the ground and pause for a moment...

Look at the person in the mirror looking back at you and say the following -

"I am very lucky to have you. As I discover more and more about you, I lovingly accept and *allow* everything that you are. Walking this path of Finding Heart with you will be amazing".

The Heart of the Matter

♥ Our minds are not our guidance system and ninety percent of the daily chatter is not coming from a higher awareness

♥ The process of Finding Heart must include the practise of dropping down into our bodies so we can get to feel our inspiration and intuition.

♥ We must learn to recognise our minds as a tool and not our master.

♥ Not being good enough' is one of our insane thought patterns that we must learn to quiet if we are going to Find Heart and become the adventure.

♥ Learn to choose which thoughts you entertain about your adventure and about yourself.

♥ The more we can accept ourselves the more we will be able to work *with* ourselves when we are following our dreams and walking our adventure.

♥ Dark places of rejection and abandonment are often created because someone else could not handle a part of us or a way in which we behave.

♥ Learning to process painful feelings and reactions and stop judgemental thoughts from running out of control is essential to leading a happy life.

♥ When we stop resisting and shift to persisting from a place of love our actions become aligned with who we really are.

The Jewel of You

Self love is the sunshine that pours onto our little plant of heart. But the concept of loving *ourselves* is not one that is high on the list of priorities in our modern society; our thoughts are outside of ourselves most of the time. We are called upon to love everyone else, our children and family expect us to love them and in fact we spend a great deal of time asking for love as much as we give it. This often comes out in the strangest ways!

Our power to direct love and acceptance toward ourselves is strong, we *can* get very honest about who we are and we *can* begin to take ourselves lightly in that acceptance. We must learn to work *with* ourselves, learn to understand from a bird's eye view the materials we are working with. It seems easier to accept the various facets of our children or family members. We can see parts of them perhaps they are not aware of, we can see how they sometimes get confused and get upset and we are there to help when they need us. We simply accept them for all that they are and their comfort and evolution is important to us. This is a wonderful gift so why not give it to ourselves as well? The truth is that compassion and love must begin with ourselves, if we are not truly accepting and loving of ourselves how can we genuinely say we are loving and accepting of others in our lives? We are just as deserving as anyone else of our love and in the context of Finding Heart it is the torch we need.

Plato once said, "Be kind, for everyone you meet is fighting a hard battle," Do you think that includes our own relationship with our self? Of course it does.

Here are some points that might help us to take self love into the real world.

- Accept our strengths and our weaknesses equally; there is strength in weakness and vice versa.
- Respect how we respond in situations, become aware of what it is we like and what it is we don't like and plan accordingly.
- Accepting there will always be days when we feel low and frightened helps us to learn not to judge ourselves quite so much.
- Give the judge the day off! Just for today let's stop feeding the judge with our internal criticism. How would someone else feel if they had to listen to our constant judgement?
- Love the plans and aspirations we have for ourselves but love and accept where we are right now and what it took to get us here.

- Love ourselves enough to get out of a job or a relationship that doesn't serve us anymore. We know when this is the case, what would you advise a friend in the same situation who you love dearly? (We can live great chunks of our lives in a lie pretending we are ok. I don't believe we should have to put up with anything our heart keeps shouting at us about. We don't have to suffer to the extent that we do if there is action we can take to make a change).
- Are some of the people we are associating with really our 'friends' are they in full support of our evolution and journey into heart? (As we make this step into getting ourselves on track some of our acquaintances will pop up as not particularly helpful with this, more on this coming later in the section 'Other people in our lives'.
- Having a respectful but strong 'No' is an important tool in the Finding Heart tool box.

Loving ourselves does not just mean learning to become aware of and accepting our faults. Oh no! It also means learning to love and become aware of the enormity of our potential and our light. This might be much harder initially and something we would rather not face.

"Our deepest fear is not that we are inadequate. Our deepest fear is that we are powerful beyond measure. It is our light, not our darkness that most frightens us. We ask ourselves, 'Who am I to be brilliant, gorgeous, talented, and fabulous?' Actually, who are you not to be? You are a child of God. Your playing small does not serve the world. There is nothing enlightened about shrinking so that other people won't feel insecure around you. We are all meant to shine, as children do. We were born to make manifest the glory of God that is within us. It's not just in some of us; it's in everyone. And as we let our own light shine, we unconsciously give other people permission to do the same. As we are liberated from our own fear, our presence automatically liberates others."

-Marianne Williamson

Isn't *that* refreshing?! There are two sides to the jewel of you. The side that is in shadow and the side that is so shiny we have to learn to step back a bit to really take it in. But it's all there and it always has been. How very exciting! We are incredible beings, the shadow just as fascinating and fertile as the light. Get interested, get intimate and get welcoming to all that you are. It's OK; we have the capacity for this. We have already thrown everything we can think of at ourselves. How about some real fascination and honour, isn't it time we stood back and marvelled at how 'jaw droppingly' amazing it is to be in the driver seat of this incredible being?

A Little Perspective...

A happy little soul was flying around one day in its formless realm of enchanted wonder. There was nothing to get done, nothing to worry about, nothing to achieve. Everything was already perfect, limitless and residing in eternal joy. It was all super lovely. One day (in the huge limitless now) the little soul met another little soul who told him about an adventure he had heard about that 'you could go on if you were brave enough'. Apparently it was a journey into a 'world' that was made up of 'opposites' like 'light & dark' and even 'good and bad'. Everyone was doing it, it was the new thing. The little souls got very excited as they began talking about and imagining what that would be like. So off they went to find out how they could get one of these 'body things'.

Having found a more experienced and learned soul who had been in this 'world' they eagerly started asking some questions.

'Oh you guys are talking about taking form, getting born, living and dying!' said the older soul. 'Yeah I've done it. Best thing I've ever done. I got back last week.'

'Really what is it? What happens, can we have a go?' The little souls enquired excitedly.

'Sure, it feels like you have disappeared for a while but in fact it just makes you forget what you are. When you come back you won't be quite the same because you will have had a great deal of 'experience'. But it can't 'hurt' you although it will feel like you can get 'hurt' when you are in it.'

The little souls looked at each other very confused and the older soul looked on with a smile.

'The best and most exciting way to describe it is to tell you about the 'body' you get given'.

'Yeah we want a body!' the little souls shouted with glee.

'The body' said the older soul enthusiastically as he knelt down in front of the little souls, 'is a form you use for the journey. It is a completely unique organic life form that begins inside someone else's body. These bodies are so incredible you can't imagine. When you are ready you are 'born' and you come out of the body you were growing in then it's your turn to go and live any adventure you want to in the world.'

'The world is another giant organic life form that has everything you need. You just won't believe what this body is and what it can do. Basically it merges with you as a soul and you can see out of it and you can control it. You can do anything you want in this world but you don't know you are in it so the amazing part is you have to learn to walk in it and learn to look after it and 'live' a life down there'.

'It's incredibly versatile but it's very fragile and if you damage it too much you will 'die' which means the game is over and you come back here. So we are programmed with this powerful respect for 'life' which means we want to preserve it all costs and we want to reproduce life. But this is the best bit; let me tell you some of the features of the body'.

'The body seems like a solid structure of what are called bones and muscle designed so you can run and play, build and create but actually it is made up of atoms which are the building blocks of matter. Matter is what everything around you will be made of. But because there are so many of them and they all bind together so tightly it makes everything 'appear' like it is solid'.

'Wow! How many atoms will we have in our bodies?' asked the little souls.

'Around 7,000,000,000,000,000,000,000,000,000. (7 octillion atoms)'.

'When you are in there it will feel like part of you is a little person sitting just behind your eyes like a conscious mind. It feels like you are tiny pulling levers and making decision that tell the body what to do. It will feel like your consciousness will have *independent existence*'.

'You can make the body learn anything, it can run, jump, dance and it will be yours. It will be unique and they are absolutely amazing. They are all different but exactly same. You will see what I mean'.

'Tell us more!' The little souls just couldn't believe what they were hearing.

'Ok' the older soul started to get just as excited and began to recall just how incredible the gift of a body really is and began to get a bit carried away.

'Nerve impulses to and from the brain travel as fast as 170 miles (274 km) per hour'.

'It takes the interaction of 72 different muscles to produce human speech'.

'Human bone is as strong as granite in supporting weight. A block of bone the size of a matchbox can support 9 tonnes –

that is four times as much as concrete can support. When you sneeze, all your bodily functions stop even your heart'.

'In the average lifetime, a person will walk the equivalent of 5 times around the equator'.

'There are 45 miles (72 km) of nerves in the skin of a human being'.

'In 30 minutes, the average body gives off enough heat (combined) to bring a half gallon of water to boil'.

The older soul was standing up again now and had noticed the little souls were just staring at him in overwhelmed shock of awesomeness but with no idea what all that meant.

'Ok', he said smiling. 'You want to know the best bit? The best bit is that it's not just your body that is unique and has all these amazing features. In fact you don't even need to know your body does all that, it just does it for you so you can get on with what you went there to do. The mix of your unique body and consciousness creates a 'character', a 'personality' and a 'purpose' and because the whole experience is made up of pole opposites it means there are things like good & bad, light and dark. These all mean we have *preferences*, likes and dislikes and we have this in-built desire that comes from our hearts to express ourselves and live our own individual adventure that *feels* the most fitting to our unique expression of consciousness'.

With that the little souls looked at each other and said simultaneously, 'Ok, were going.'

Who wouldn't have a go at that? OK none of us know where we have come from or if there is a 'formless realm of enchanted wonder'. But all the description and facts about us that you have just read are real. What a crying shame it would be to spend the majority of the time complaining about the particular body we got or how the personality turned out. Why on earth would we really want to sit there doing that with a unique adventure waiting?

II

The Sun and the Soil

The Power of Feeling Good.

"Some of the worst things in my life never actually happened."
Mark Twain

We know intuitively that life is good; we are programmed to preserve it and to reproduce it. It is when we feel good that great things happen and when great things happen we feel good. Finding Heart is a good feeling.

So what we are going to do now is learn a game and feeling good is the aim. Everything works better when we feel good. We can choose to feel good most of the time, no matter what happens it is only very rarely that we need to feel awful for any long period of time. We cannot control ourselves to the extent where we can dictate how we are going to feel about something at any one time. That is the wonder of this experience but we can *choose* to feel good much of the time. Our core feels good, our hearts feel good. There is good feeling in us all and when we acknowledge this and allow ourselves to let go of even half of the stuff we insist on carrying around with us we open the door to a source of wellbeing that is always available. Are you laughing at the page right now? Exclaiming that *choosing* to feel good is a ridiculous suggestion? 'There are too many other feelings happening to simply choose feeling good!' I understand, however read on and just for a laugh give this a try to see what happens.

An act of creating space for our heart to breathe means making room in our lives so we can listen to what it is we really want. Finding Heart is predominantly about growing the feeling of feeling good. The feel good game is practising and committing to feeling good whatever is going on. Initially it is in fact easier than you might think. It is possible to make a personal decision and commitment to feeling good on a continuous basis and you may always remember the moment when you first make the decision to do this yourself. This will soon become the moment when you realise you have a choice and you *can* actually choose.

There are always things in our lives that will irritate us and there will always be hard things to process such as losing loved ones. We may notice that our default setting is usually to associate the things that happen in our day with things that are wrong. We are problem solvers but there are many things in our lives that cannot be solved today. But we still think them through and try to solve them as though we can often with a feeling of helplessness. This is a program we will notice we have running. We assume that if we think about something for long enough eventually we will make the problem disappear. But generally most of the time all we are achieving is to make ourselves *feel* uncomfortable and inevitably bad.

So this is about making a decision to just simply feel good. When is a good time to do this? The best time is when you finish reading this sentence, but there are a few things we need to put in place first. To get an idea look across the room or the view from where you are sitting, just stop for a second and drop your awareness into your body, relax your body and settle into feeling in your body. Allow your awareness to fall down into the base of your abdomen and relax everything as you go down. Relax your shoulders and feel the sensation of your body letting go. Now smile. No matter what is going on in your life today, just smile. Begin to appreciate the moment you are experiencing right now as literally just that, a moment in the great history of the world. Smile at the wonder of the fact we are both sitting on a planet spinning in space around a sun in a galaxy in the middle of the magnificence of the universe. Picture the wonder of nature and how the position of this planet in our solar system happens to miraculously support complex life, it so easily couldn't and we might never be here. Think right now of the dance of activity happening across the world, the actual reality of what is going on and then smile again. This is the beginning of a new start.

Did you allow yourself to feel good then? You can do it, even if you are wracked with worry stop again and ask yourself which of those problems was *actually happening* in the moment you read the previous paragraph?

For the moment we are just going to be feeling 'unreasonably' happy. Imagining wonders may only keep us distracted for a short period of time. Then after this the game will begin. For the purposes of this exercise and hopefully beyond, feeling good is going to become our dominant intention. We are simply going to get in the moment and feel good. The thoughts and the chatter in our minds will soon start up again and we will forget. So let the game begin! When we follow a painful thought process and begin feeding ourselves with discomfort we are going to learn that we are able to stop it. This is what we are going to be practising in the game.

We will notice that 90% of the time we are in fact following relatively pointless thought processes. These might be judgements upon ourselves, or unnecessary worry and concern. Or we may be taking the fact it is raining personally. We may be driving and moaning about the way someone else is driving. We may by listening to the radio and complaining to ourselves that the government is not doing its job properly.

If negative thought processes seem to be our default setting we are now going to change that to the positive. Feeling good usually only happens when we are affected by outside influences or we *happen* to be feeling good. In reality our own happiness is not at the mercy of the outside world and the people in it. I agree that things *seem* to happen to us that make us feel unhappy but in fact it is often the thought processes we choose that make us unhappy and *being* unhappy breeds more unhappiness. Like Qui-Gon said to Anakin during Star Wars "Our focus determines our reality." If you haven't seen or heard of Star Wars my point is, have you noticed that we colour the world with how we are feeling? If we feel good we tend to notice things accordingly and vice versa. In my experience the effects run quite deeply and the choice to feel good is essential to the unfolding of our adventure and getting back into our heartfelt flow. It kick starts the life we are looking for into our reality.

Very often we are following negative thoughts and worrying about things that will probably never happen. But we follow a thought association through to our own conclusion, decide that this is the inevitable route of things and then act as though it is now actually happening. We put ourselves through an awful lot of unnecessary pain. What do you think would start to happen if we changed that thought association to a positive one and then followed that through to its conclusion?

Perhaps we can understand why we seem to have a default setting of worry. Modern life is stressful. We have mortgages, bills, school fees and the constant bombardment of the media urging us to consume more and look for our happiness through material wealth. The system of society may well seem to be keeping us in debt and under control but if we are living in a free country there is nothing stopping us from living our adventure and freeing *ourselves*.

A conscious choice to feel good is the way to this and it is great fun learning to feel unreasonably good. It is possible to feel good when there is no apparent reason to feel good. We can still think through our problems and concerns but we can do so with a chosen base feeling of good rather than despair. Our inner self is inherently happy and re-learning to feel the peace and sanity in our hearts really helps to un-clutter our inner lives. Essentially we are gentle organic creatures with simple needs and in the simplicity is our strength, our guidance and our purpose. We complicate our lives unmercifully and we put enormous pressure on ourselves. The majority of this pressure is not ours. It might be from our parents who felt they were doing the best for us. Or it is from society and it is from the voices and programs we have developed along the way. If the majority of the pressure is not inherent to us then returning to our natural state of feel good as often as we can remember is nowhere near as difficult as you would think.

From the stillness we all have inside we can allow ourselves to feel the contentment and joy in our own hearts; the truth in ourselves. Like the self we know when we are on holiday; when we have taken care of everything back home so we can relax. When we have turned off our phones and switched off all our devices for two weeks. When we really let go lying in the sunshine, we *allow* ourselves to feel good. We know all our stress is waiting for us when we get home again but we just switch it off for the moment and relax. To feel good now we do not need to unravel all the misgivings of our past. We don't need to go into years of therapy to try to uncover the reason for our unhappiness and we don't need to go on holiday. We are going to bypass this now with an acceptance of all that we are and the decision to simply feel happy right now. Regardless of what is going on.

The decision to consciously choose feeling good as our default setting is a bit like reaching down into a box and pulling off items of clutter from a light underneath. When we are in the light of balance we are in the right place to work. Sometimes it is as simple as relaxing our face into a gentle smile to relax the body into the now and "taa daa!" There is our feel good heart again.

The Sphere of You

So we will begin the game soon but before we do there are two sections here that contain key bits of information that we can take with us. This one was born from a great deal of work that took place between myself and one of my teachers when I first started working with the Feel Good Game. In my experience downloading this as an idea can be an incredibly freeing experience that helps us to love and accept ourselves and it is very useful for the game. In essence it invites us to remember that we are *not* only the light.

Imagine a sphere popping off your body from the back, front, top and bottom so you are now inside a beautiful human sized hamster ball of energy. The ball is invisible and silent but it is always there. Inside this ball is where all of us takes place. It is the ball of allowance. We can let anyone come and stand next to us, hug us or touch us but no-one is actually ever inside our sphere apart from us. They have one too but ours and everything that happens inside of ours is exclusive to us. It can be thought of as our energy field or like an aura.

Now imagine the sphere as the Ying Yang symbol. There is light and dark and we are in the middle in balance. If we go far enough into the light we will find the dark and if we go far enough into the dark we will find the light. The light and the dark in the sphere is *our* very essence; we all have both polarities inside us and in our sphere of allowance we never deny the fact that we have difficult feelings dark urges and a happy and unhappy nature. Stay with me we are nearly done on this but if we can really grasp this, it is very liberating and it's vital to making the game we are playing much easier.

See the sphere as our judgement free environment and it will cater for anything we can possibly conjure up; it is designed to house everything that passes through us. So when we are playing our feel good game we are entirely welcoming to anything that comes into our sphere of awareness. Feeling good is not about pretending we are a fuzzy ball of light that never has difficult feelings. Sometimes we are home to ancient thought unbounded by time from the darkest recesses of goodness knows where. Equally we are not negative, unhappy and dark all the time and it is always our choice what we entertain and *feed*. We are everything and everything is represented in us. We are light and we are shadow and if we try to play the Feel Good Game insisting we are only the light we will end up out of whack with reality. Sooner or later the shadow will engulf us to bring us back into balance. Feel completely safe in the sphere; all is welcome in there, no-one else shares it so we can get very intimate with ourselves and acknowledge all that passes, dances and sometimes tears through it. The light is not better than the dark and vice versa, they both just *are*.

Remember, "Life will never throw anything at us that we can't handle".

Ok that's quite enough on that, how is your facial expression right now? Has it curled up on one side in disdain as though you've just seen a cat coughing up a fur ball? Don't worry, have a play with the idea of the sphere, the main thing to come away with here is to acknowledge the reality of our nature. In that acceptance we can keep it real when it comes to the Feel Good Game.

Silence, Stillness, Power & Love

Here are some tools that we will need for the game and they are the words *Silence, Stillness* and *Power*. There is something magical about these words when used in a certain way. They become a way to stop the ongoing process of thought association and the feelings we induce that throw us off base. Quite simply we are saying each particular word to a part of our body. Give this a try and remember to use it when the mind starts up with negativity and affecting feelings in the body.

Silence – Place your hand on your forehead and say to your mind the word 'SILENCE'. Feel your thoughts silence.

Stillness – Place your hand on your chest and say to your heart the word 'STILLNESS'. Feel the feelings in your body relax.

Power – Place your hand below your stomach and say the word 'POWER'. Is there an action that needs to be taken in this moment?

Try this and keep practising it. It's very effective in the beginnings of overwhelm and when we catch ourselves stomping down a negative thought pattern. It sounds too simple but try it and *allow* the mind to be quiet and the heart still. When we notice the difference we see how agitated we can allow ourselves to become. Being agitated on a regular basis is not conducive to feeling the heartfelt and contented flow in us that becomes our adventure. So we can help ourselves by turning down the noise around and inside ourselves.

This is in fact one of a few techniques we are going to learn that helps us to find our natural state of calm and *feel good* which of course is what Finding Heart is based in. This one is just very useful for the day to day process of keeping ourselves feeling good and it's great for the Feel Good Game. When this technique becomes second nature to us we will begin to ask ourselves what action we now need to take that is in alignment with our hearts. This is where the Power comes in. When we silence and still ourselves we may notice there is something else needed and that may be to take action. Something we need to do for ourselves that may be as simple as leaving a room and having five minutes to ourselves.

The additional but equally important sentences we will be using to help keep our sphere processing and working well are those magical three words, 'I Love You' and 'I forgive you'. This may feel a little strange directing these to ourselves and if that is the case then right there is the evidence we need to be saying it regularly.

When we have helped our self release negative thoughts, difficult feelings or judgements; using these two phrases can be very beneficial to bring ourselves back into balance. It helps to acknowledge that we are doing our best, we are learning and most importantly that we honour ourselves again.

It is applied in the same way we might say it to someone we love when we are hugging them, we simply close our eyes, smile and say to ourselves 'I love you, I forgive you'.

These are powerful sentences and filling our own sphere with this type of energy and intention is incredibly nurturing and creates a fertile environment when we are actively bringing something as special as our adventure through ourselves. I invite you to get used to saying these words to yourself and noting the types of reactions and sensations they induce.

So now we have a loving sphere of allowance with silence, stillness and power in our toolbox we can begin the 40 day feel good game!

The Heart of the Matter

♥ Finding Heart is a good feeling.

♥ Finding Heart is predominantly about growing the feeling of feeling good.

♥ It is possible to feel good when there is no apparent reason to feel good.

♥ To feel good now we do not need to unravel all the misgivings of our past.

♥ Sometimes it is as simple as relaxing our face into a gentle smile to relax the body into the now.

♥ Feeling good is not about pretending we are a fuzzy ball of light that never has difficult feelings.

♥ Life will never throw anything at us that we can't handle

The 40 Day Feel Good Game

So the purpose of this game is to feel good. This may sound obvious but we have to stay on the ball with this because it's very easy to slip into negativity before we realise where we are again. This game is best played during our normal day to day routine. I am very aware that right now you may not be feeling on top of the world. Perhaps you are feeling the worst you have ever felt and I am not suggesting that you suddenly need to be clear of all your problems. I am inviting you to bring on a good feeling regardless of what is going on for you. At first it may well have no grounding whatsoever and may be the opposite to what the circumstances of your life are indicating. If you feel like you have a responsibility to be unhappy at the moment because it seems as though it will make things right again, I understand. I invite you to let go of that just for today. This choice is not about letting life walk all over us or giving in and pretending that the injustice in life is ok. It is about regenerating the natural ability we have to take control again of the environment within our own bodies. Not necessarily having a reason to feel good to begin with is a way to enter the game.

You will still be playing the game after you have finished reading this book and you will still be playing it as you start taking action from the work you are going to be doing with your adventure in the coming sections. The bespoke state of feel good you will discover will drive your adventure and it will be the way in to the wonderful feeling of being back in your flow.

Remember the source of power we all hold in our hearts is incredible and when we are living in alignment with it the world literally changes colour. So take a chance and let's play. When we begin to get good at this game we begin to get used to the feeling of Finding Heart. This feeling is a sense of knowing and an inner contentment that we begin to make decisions from and to use as our guidance system.

The trick to the game is to find the feel good feeling that is authentic to *you*. Why is it forty days? We do this for forty days because when we hold a particular state *as best as we can* for forty days we can actually start to become it and embody it on a cellular level. Don't worry by the time you reach forty days you will know the happiness that is authentic to you and you can't get this wrong. All that will happen is in six weeks time you will be feeling good the majority of the time. You can easily change back; you will have a choice as we always do. Forty days may seem like a long time but during that period we are going to be feeling good, which is what we are all trying to achieve anyway.

Open up the calendar in your diary or on your phone and write '40 Day FGG - Day 1` then count 40 days and put a note on the last day so you can keep track of where you are. Let's bring that feeling on again now. Smile, relax your body and just allow yourself to feel good. Stand up, shake your hands at the side of your body jump up and down, take a deep breath in, stand still again and breathe out a deep sigh of relief.

Say to yourself:

Just for today I am going to let go of worry.

I am going to *allow* all the feelings that come through my sphere then I will let go and return to my natural state of feeling good.

When I get overwhelmed I will stop and use the techniques that work best to balance me again. (There are a series of techniques coming soon we can incorporate into the game).

We do not need to be outwardly extrovert and try to make everyone else around us cheer up unless of course that feels right for us to do that. It is a personal choice to feel good. This becomes our default setting. Perhaps you are about to go downstairs to an angry spouse or partner, tired children and a really untidy kitchen. Either way you are in now, feeling good is now your *personal* choice it is a game you are playing with *yourself.* If we can hold a state for forty days it stays with us.

Now there are some guidelines and the reality will be that it simply isn't possible to hold one particular state for long periods of time. The game is to return to feeling good at every opportunity. When we find we simply can't do that it doesn't mean we have failed. This is a game so it has rules and we will look at those now. When we read "Just for today" that means *this* day within the forty days. Remember we take everything one day at a time.

1. **Just for today we do not hold a negative thought process for a second longer than we have become aware of it.**

Have fun with this. When someone pulls out in front of you next time you are driving you will respond as usual. But then stop, 'Silence' and smile. Holding this good feeling has now become your greatest goal. Don't let anyone snatch this from you so easily! *Stop* the negative thought pattern that wants to strike itself into action next time something goes wrong. Don't repress or judge the feelings but don't extenuate them with negative thoughts. Allow the feelings to be there, acknowledge the thought then *let go*. Don't give anything power over you. Just for today you will not be a victim of any kind. Remember the motivation to do this is the pursuit of your adventure, there is purpose behind this.

2. **Just for today we let go of the need to be right.**

There is a great saying that says 'You can be right or you can be happy.' Needing to be right seems to be a natural human need. Perhaps it helps us to form our opinions and it helps us to understand who we are. Perhaps it was necessary when we were growing up. But have you noticed the insane tennis match we play as grown ups? It's painful and we all do it.

Not today though, today we let go of the need to be right. Are we really so insecure that we continuously need the experience of having our opinions and feelings affirmed by someone else telling us we are right? We will notice that most of the time people don't like to tell us we are right because they want to be right! One love, but the game will never end apart from ending in frustration. Let go of this fruitless task. Remember it's only for today. Then after the forty days we can go back to being right if we insist, but for now it's against the rules.

3. We do not talk about the Feel Good Game until we have completed the 40 days!

At this point we are growing a little plant, our feel good plant. We talk more on this later but if we start sharing what we are doing we are exposing our little plant or seedling to some dangerous weather. Let it grow, let it settle and find its roots. By day 41 it will bend to bad weather if you decide to keep it.

4. Just for today we make a commitment to stop the analysis of ourselves; we accept everything that we are wherever we are right now.

This is an important rule. Rules are a stiff word but it is just a game, like life. The more we can learn to take ourselves less seriously the easier we will get on. They say the reason angels can fly is because they take themselves lightly! Let go of the urge to fathom what you think is wrong with you. I know we have discussed this already but if we try to cure all of our wounds with endless analysis and discussion before we begin to live our lives we will not get anywhere. So when things go wrong and we get upset *please* let go of the addiction to self judgement and loathing. This is a critical part to the feel good game; silence and smile! Remember to say the words 'I love you and I forgive you' *to yourself*. Be aware that the base states of despair, melancholy and anger are all highly addictive. They all have their place their function and their 'pay off', but sulking is a choice and one we will not be making during these forty days. Think of this analysis and these lower states as a hole in the road. If we keep following the same thought pattern like a particular road (the one with the hole in it) we are going to fall in the same hole again and again. Instead we choose not to walk down that particular road altogether by entertaining positive thought patterns.

Did you know the average human being thinks around 70,000 thoughts each day and 90% of those are the thoughts we had yesterday? If a high percentage of those are not making us feel good and keep sending us into the same hole then isn't it time to start choosing different thoughts?

5. Just for today we speak and play consciously.

Before we speak we take a moment to think about the flavour of what is about to come out of our mouths. During these forty days we will be making a conscious effort to think highly of ourselves. This means we do not put ourselves down when we are in conversation, even in jest. We can go back to it if we want after the forty days but for now we are going to get into the habit of thinking and speaking highly of ourselves. Try to speak honestly and kindly. This is quite challenging because often people in our lives expect us to respond and act in a certain way. If the type of interaction we are having with friends and family is derogatory for both parties it is OK to change our reactions and responses. Even if it is in jest start to bring some awareness into it; look for the intention behind what we are about to say. Begin to notice the things we say about ourselves and about other people. Lying, putting ourselves down and speaking on autopilot is not Finding Heart.

6. **Just for today we choose not to drop energy when someone puts us down, play instead or walk away!**

Often when we begin to feel great we begin to hold ourselves in high esteem. That's great news! This is what we want to be feeling. We are looking to raise our vibration, our level of happiness and our feeling of well being. Perhaps we might begin to change the way we dress and these changes can be threatening to friends and family. So if they put us down we don't match that frequency, instead we maintain feeling highly of ourselves and play in our response. We might do a little dance with a big smile on our face and say something like "I know! I'm just feeling great today and had to put a suit on!" This is also great practise for strengthening our relationship with our values.

7. **We keep our boundaries in place. Just because we are happy doesn't mean we get walked over.**

When I first made my commitment to play the Feel Good Game it felt like nothing could break my flow. Quite soon into the game I can remember I came home to discover my flat mate at the time had gone into my room and given a pair of my thermals to a friend of his who needed something warm to wear to a Yoga class. My thermals are very personal to me as I use them as pyjamas in the winter. At the time I was learning the Feel Good Game and it felt like the thing to do was pretend I didn't care so I could carry on feeling good. But soon the feel good feeling turned to frustration and I realised that *what was most important to me* in that scenario was that my personal items were respected as private to me. So the action I needed to take was to explain this in a way to my flat mate that acknowledged his need to look after his friend at the time and to let him know that my thermals were personal to me and I needed that to be respected.

In doing this one of my values had emerged in relation to my personal space which came to light when I asked myself the question "what is most important to me right now?" Soon I was back on track and feeling good again. It isn't always easy to act in alignment with our values because it means having faith our heart knows what is best for us but it is important if we want to end up with a consistent feel good that we can sustain. (I recommend making notes on your values page through the Feel Good Game, it will really help you).

The final yet one of the most important rules is –

8. **We acknowledge on Day 1 that there will be periods during the 40 days when we will not be feeling good!**

We don't know what is going to be passing through us and what we will encounter during the forty days, sometimes it will seem like nothing works and we can't go on. This is perfectly normal! Every human being on the planet has days like this but when we are in the middle of the Feel Good Game and we have a total breakdown it can feel much worse because it feels like we have failed. It does *not* mean we have failed! Humans are ephemeral in other words always changing and in these instances our job is to simply allow whatever needs to pass through pass through and as soon as we can we help it we let go. Letting go is a very freeing experience.

We can consciously provide ourselves with the best chance we can by being patient and by finding the courage to drop the judgement and come back to where we left off when we have recovered. When we allow ourselves to feel good again we will often find the worst will be over much quicker than our thoughts seem to threaten. We'll have a new viewpoint to see clearly again.

To conclude we remember that during a game of any kind there can't be a chance of unrivalled success otherwise it's not much of a game. Any player that simply throws his or her hands in the air and never comes back when it goes wrong is simply taking everything way too seriously. There is no getting it wrong or failing with this it is simply finding the courage to accept whatever has just happened, find a solution if we need to, *let it go* and *allow* ourselves to come back to the authentic state of feel good that is real for us right now. How many problems or past grievances have been solved or improved with long periods of sulking, worry or blame? Every moment is a chance to continue again in the Feel Good Game.

Here are the rules and guidelines again in summary –

1. Just for today we do not hold a negative thought process for a second longer than we have become aware of it.
2. Just for today we let go of the need to be right.
3. We do not talk about the feel good game until we have completed the 40 days!
4. Just for today we make a commitment to stop the analysis of ourselves; we accept everything that we are wherever we are right now.
5. Just for today we speak & play consciously.
6. Just for today we choose not to drop energy when someone puts us down, play instead or walk away!
7. We keep our boundaries in place. Just because we are happy doesn't mean we get walked over.

8. We acknowledge on Day 1 that there will be periods during the 40 days when we will not be feeling good!

The game will create stages to illustrate what we think is a natural state of feel good and the feel good that is really ours. This is where it gets interesting and so important for Finding Heart. We have an idea of what we think happiness ought to be for us compared to what it actually is. This will come through the experience of the forty days. You will know you have it when you find you can stay in it with more and more stability as you go about your day to day life. We find that more and more of our life begins to settle into this new frequency we are choosing. The cheerfulness in our demeanour begins to link with the feeling of happiness in our body, this is Finding Heart. Play in the game, try being happy in whatever way feels right to you. If it means being animated, extrovert and expressive then this is what you must go with. If it means being calm, peaceful and attentive then go with that. Find the happiness within you, the happiness that is not dependent on outside events, material things or circumstance. *Be unreasonably happy.*

When we find the authentic state of feel good we start applying this to what we have written in the commitment exercise and then we will be able to see whether our adventure and the fashion in which we are bringing it into reality is *truly aligned with our values*. Choosing this natural state in my experience means the heart doesn't have quite so much to work to do to get us to where we want to be.

We will be challenged during the 40 days. Things will happen that will make it difficult for us to maintain our feel good. People will present things to us that require us to respond in a way that honours what we value. This is exactly what we need. To really develop a strong and authentic heartfelt flow again we are going to need our boundaries challenged in order for us to identify what is most important to us.

Our values become a little easier to spot during a commitment to feeling good. We begin to become more sensitive to what we like. When something throws us off balance we go back to the question "What is most important to me about this"? Then we know if we need to act or speak to bring ourselves or the situation back into balance. Feeling good is not mindless, it is attentive and authentic. It is poised, ready to engage and ready to respond accordingly. It is respectful, powerful and the more we practise the more our days begin to fill with our heartfelt flow again.

So have fun and enjoy this game as you take it with you to work on your adventure. Write your progress, discoveries and insights in your notebook or diary as you go through the forty days. When you get stuck or something goes wrong it is because you are discovering something! Everything will be leading to the feel good authenticity of you and your adventure. Sounds like Finding Heart to me ☺

The Myth of Personal Development

Now that we are actively involved with the Feel Good Game and about to look at more techniques and courses of action, we need to discuss something important. To do that let's look at a definition of personal development:

'Personal development includes activities that improve awareness and identity, develop talents and potential, build human capital and facilitate employability, enhance quality of life and contribute to the realization of dreams and aspirations.'

Personal development is also a huge industry with some trainings and seminars costing tens of thousands. By no means am I suggesting that these courses are fake and don't work because I have personally attended many of them. But we must walk into the arena of personal development with a sense of perspective and reality.

Personal development is a wonderful medium to help us grow, resolve previous misunderstandings or traumas and to generate an authentic awareness about ourselves. But there is no course or training out there that is going to cure all our wounds or make us eternally happy in one fell swoop. This would bypass the very nature of being human since it is down to us to evolve. No matter what it says on the tin, in the few weeks following the course or training it is highly likely we will return to how we felt before. The only way we can sustain the changes we felt during the training is *if we take action.*

Seminars, books and trainings trigger insight into new ways of looking at things, triggers that can start new and important neuro-pathways in our brains. New ways to think and cathartic processes that help us release and shift blocked emotion and negative thought patterns. They help us to shine a light into a dark space we may have previously had no conscious awareness of before and in my opinion this is supremely important for our happiness and development. But there is no magic cure. Even if we go and live in the mountains with a guru for twenty years the work is down to *us*. There is nothing out there that is going to make the change for us. Regardless of how expensive it is, who is teaching it or where in the world it is held.

Refusing to act until the personal development training has 'fixed our wounds' is going to get very costly. Our wounding and our ego are here for a purpose and they are part of the bigger picture. We have to have the polarity of dark and light; good and bad to exist. Destruction, mishap and disaster are a natural part of us as much as they are a part of nature. They clear out the old and create anew. I am not disputing the great stories of awakening and enlightenment but if we want a great story to tell to that old person on our death bed we must get involved *now*. If we want a personal development book, training or technique to have an effect we must *actively apply* it into who we are as an individual.

Thinking new content through, reading about and sitting in seminars will give us the tools but nothing was ever completed by simply reading the instructions and then sitting on the tool box. We must pick up our tools with heart and mind in alignment ready to make mistakes, ready to learn and ready to keep going until we have built the first platform of our adventure from which we can stand to see how we build the next.

We must break any addiction we have to personal development in the hope it will magically do the work for us simply through reading or being present at a training. Or that we feel we must use it to change the very nature of who we are before we begin to lead the life we want. So with the content of this book it would be my greatest wish for you to get involved if you haven't already. Use the techniques we are about to learn to process difficult feelings, blocks and troublesome thoughts. Try them out and use them to maintain and grow a respectful loving acceptance of yourself. Use them to clear the ground ahead to live the adventure authentic to you and in turn you can nurture the good feelings that will emerge as a result. Play the Feel good Game and treat yourself when you have reached the 40th day. If we want to see progress and change in our lives it means we are going to have to get out of the seats and onto the field.

Getting in Shape for Our Adventure

When we commit to feeling good and Finding Heart sometimes we *may* need to address some of our personal habits in regards to what we are ingesting. I have put the word 'may' in italics up there because it is not always the case and if we really need guidance with this the best indicator is how we are personally feeling. I am including this section because I am committed to your progress and it wouldn't feel right to me if I didn't, especially because I know the world of too many toxins and I also know the world of going too far the other way as well .

Our commitment is to get a clear signal on how we are feeling about things on a daily basis and to take action according to how we are feeling. Some people may be able to play the Feel Good Game really well and make excellent progress with their adventure quite intoxicated in one way or another. I cannot make judgement because we are all unique. But it may be the case that someone else with the same bodily environment cannot differentiate between their own feelings and the feelings that might be happening as a result of being intoxicated. Some of us can drink ourselves silly and function perfectly well the following day and some of us can suffer feelings of depression the following day, so we need to take responsibility for this ourselves.

One of the most debilitating things I have found that makes me very tired and unhappy is eating badly, drinking to excess on a regular basis and not exercising. But that is how I am and this may not be the case for you. So this section is simply an invitation to see *if* this needs addressing; only you know if it does. If our habits are not supporting us and we want to see a change we are going to have to make the changes ourselves. What is so fantastic about this life is that in every moment we have the chance to start anew if we need to.

Simple changes like this can count a great deal towards finding ourselves. But what is most important is that we are not judging our behaviour or our habits. If you are the type of person who can function perfectly well mildly intoxicated or find it a great benefit to take the edge off with well chosen intoxicants then under no circumstances do I intend to worry you.

It can be frustrating when we are told we need to alter things as necessary and personal such as the way we are eating or what we are putting into our body. As if we don't have enough to think about already! Can we at least not have our eating habits as sacred and undisturbed? This is why I am being sensitive and empathising with you. Especially because continued negative self judgement is highly toxic in itself and under no circumstances do I want to induce that. But as I say I am committed to your progress so if you know your behaviour is not serving you or equally if you *are* judging your behaviour unnecessarily then hopefully this section will have highlighted this for you.

To be in alignment with who we are, to allow ourselves to be us and to live in our flow requires an intimate relationship with ourselves. It means that we are going to have to be able to hear ourselves properly and by 'hearing ourselves' I mean being able to feel into our bodies and hear our truth. Abuse of toxins and bad food can make our bodies sluggish and they can also make it noisy with artificially induced feelings that can make Finding Heart more difficult.

If you have got this far with reading this book it says to me you are opening up to yourself and committed to living the adventure in you. So I am going to ask you a few questions that I invite you to consider and answer honestly in your notebook.

1. How you are feeling on a day to day basis? Do you feel clear headed or do you feel toxic and fatigued?
2. Can you compare this to another point in your life where you have felt better?
3. If you can remember, what were your ingestion habits like then?
4. Do you feel your eating habits are serving you or not?
5. Do you feel you are drinking too much? (Only you know what your own system will process and cope with).
6. Take a moment to describe your relationship to recreational drugs? (I would include sugar & caffeine to this list).
7. Do you feel you have healthy moderation in your diet and behaviour in general?

8. Do you feel you may be repressing yourself on a
   regular basis with food or intoxicants?

How do these questions make you feel? Did you feel some
guilt coming up when you began to read them? Please make
sure you are not making any unnecessary judgements on
yourself based on other people's opinions. However please
check in with yourself to see if your feelings are indicating that
a change of some sort may need to happen. Perhaps you have
been intending to make some changes already. As we commit
to this new life choice of living *our* lives and embarking on our
own path it all starts with listening to these feelings of warning
and hints of direction. Everything in us wants to fall into flow,
we are a part of natures flow and the wonder of being human
means we have a conscious choice to be alignment with it or
not. The value of being honest with ourselves is taking our
intuition seriously.

Above all remember it is your body and your mind and it is
your right to do whatever you feel is right for them. In my
experience it is simply not authentic for me to become
obsessive about being healthy. I feel that becoming obsessed
with healthy living is itself an imbalance. I feel the most
benefit comes from listening to our own bodies and creating
bespoke habits. When we get healthy impulses to eat
particular fresh produce when we walk around a supermarket
it is an indication our bodies need it, taking action to feed
ourselves accordingly is an act of love.

Equally some of my most creative moments are at a party
when I'm slightly intoxicated! When I feel the urge I will enjoy
a few drinks with my friends, maybe the following day I will
eat a big fried breakfast with maybe another couple of drinks
at lunch time. I may then go to the cinema and have ice cream.

Then that evening it will be a pizza and a couple more drinks. However if I then continue this pattern into the following day I know this is out of flow for me. I am not listening to my body anymore and quite frankly I wouldn't enjoy it if I continued with the same behaviour. I feel great as I go back to my current project and feel my body clearing itself again. But if I deny myself a couple of days like that every once in a while this is not listening to my needs either. Each of us has a balance and when we take care to notice the little feelings of impulse to stop or start something we are gradually building and strengthening the communication channels with our hearts.

Before we move on I would like to say something further on changing diet or cutting something out. In my experience it needs to be done gradually. You may be able to cut something out immediately and finally but for some it can be a shock to the body. If we remove something entirely over night it can have quite an adverse effect. Get some advice and take it one day at a time. I find it especially difficult if I just make a mental list of everything I *can't* have and then walk round the supermarket as normal. I like to find help that shows me what I can have. Take the time to make the change properly. Remember we left any sticks we like to beat ourselves with right at the beginning.

If there is a reason for drinking too much which may be reflective of other imbalances in our life then processing the feelings underneath is the way through. If we are pretty unhappy because we are drinking and taking drugs to repress and to cope then the changes we make in our lives in accordance with our values will help to shift us out of the habit. I know this only too well and there have been unhappy periods in my life when I have been under the cloud of continuous intoxication. Being an alcoholic is a different matter and having had a very close friend who was a full blown alcoholic I have learned this is a condition that needs specialised help which I advise you seek if this also applies to you. No-one needs to know you are getting help, go for it. You can do it.

I have also worked with people whose unhappiness is fuelling a drinking/drug habit but when I have helped to get them back in alignment with their values and to begin living their adventure being overly intoxicated on a regular basis becomes annoying for them. The mind loses its sharpness and the body gets tired and when they get excited and focussed they simply forget to buy more alcohol or get intoxicated again. Our aim here is to be honest with ourselves, allowing the truth in us to emerge is all the fuel we need to make a change.

Other Outside Interference

Again without making any judgements or suggesting we need to judge any of the following, I will extend this discussion to have a quick check in about other outside interference. Do we need to think about particular things we are exposing ourselves to on TV for example? Is there anything that might be having a negative impact on us such as soap dramas or TV shows? Just because we are recommended something does not necessarily mean it is appropriate for us.

What about bad press in the newspapers and radio? If the body flinches at something, make a choice as to whether it is flagging up a value that needs acknowledging or if it something we don't need to expose ourselves to. If we fancy watching a movie that is gruesome and disturbing quickly check in and ask if we need those sorts of images and emotional responses running through our system at this time. Any habits we have that are based in negativity and cloud our system *may* need to come into our awareness for review.

Some may be habits we have as a nation or even as a civilisation but we always have an individual choice to assess them. Remember the base states of emotion are addictive and addictions are sneaky!

Thank you for staying with me on these two sections, perhaps it has uncovered some changes you would like to make and perhaps it hasn't. If it has record your progress with them in your notebook and add anything useful you would like to take with you. Still friends? ☺ Let's move on..

The Heart of the Matter

- ♥ The bespoke state of feel good you will discover will drive your adventure and it will be the way in to the wonderful feeling of being back in your flow.
- ♥ The trick to the Feel Good Game is to find the feel good feeling that is authentic to *you*.
- ♥ Let go of the addiction to self judgement and loathing.
- ♥ Be aware that the base states of despair, melancholy and anger are all highly addictive.
- ♥ Get into the habit of thinking and speaking highly of yourself.
- ♥ When we allow ourselves to feel good again we will often find the worst will be over much quicker than our thoughts seem to threaten.
- ♥ If we want a personal development book, training or technique to have an effect we must *actively apply* it into who we are as an individual.
- ♥ Abuse of toxins and bad food can make our bodies sluggish and they can also make it noisy with artificially induced feelings that can make Finding Heart more difficult.
- ♥ Any habits we have that are based in negativity and cloud our system *may* need to come into our awareness for review.

Healing Our Way to Finding Heart

Our work here is about consciously choosing to support the truth and innocence that we were born with. By *choosing* to feel good as our new default setting we are in turn tending to the earth that supports the green shoots of our true and happy self. So the more we can nurture our truth based in feeling good whilst we process the weeds of negativity the more we can allow ourselves to be us. This is the power we are looking to take with us on our own days of adventure. The system of self is wonderfully intricate and operating on many levels and like all great engineering it will flourish with a powerful energy source. This brings us to a great advantage we can give ourselves if it is one that feels right.

I'm sure you have heard of Reiki. I have an incredible person in my life who gives me Reiki on a regular basis; she has been a powerful inspiration for me and one of the finest teachers I have met. Her patience and consistency over the years has assisted my journey in ways I cannot put into words. I feel very blessed and supremely grateful to know her and it was our work together that led to the writing of this book.

Of all the alternative therapies I have come across and tried, Reiki is an incredible fuel for adventures. It clears out the old and it gains us direct insight into what we're doing and where we are going. It aligns us with our hearts desire and language. A good Reiki healer can also read where we are and will help us to see where we are going. Sometimes they speak to us whilst they are giving Reiki and almost like a Clairvoyant they can 'read' us. This keeps us tuned like a piano and we definitely sound better as a result. Reiki is a way of keeping the Chi or energy flowing through our bodies.

So what on earth does this really mean and what is Reiki anyway?

Reiki is a Japanese technique that promotes healing. It is given by "laying on hands" and is based on the idea that an unseen "life force energy" flows through us and is what causes us to be alive. If one's "life force energy" is low, then we are more likely to get ill or feel stress. If it is high, we are more capable of being happy and healthy.

The word Reiki is made of two Japanese words - Rei which means "God's Wisdom or the Higher Power" and Ki which is "life force energy". So Reiki is actually "spiritually guided life force energy."

If this sounds a bit too spiritual for you then think of your body as an electrical channel. According to NASA we can produce up to 1630 watts of electricity when we sprint! Our nervous systems run on electrical impulses so think of Chi or energy as natural electricity that flows through specific points in our bodies. When we have a regular flow of this it helps us to heal and progress. It can help us to vibrate on a frequency that is more in tune with our purpose and helps us to be more open to our own inspiration. It helps to keep our thoughts from overwhelming us and keeps our bodies and mind in alignment. Personally I have found Reiki treatments all over the world during my travels and teachings because of how much it energises the journey. It also helps to shift old programs we have running and can help to leave old patterns of life and behaviour behind that no longer serve us.

Reiki treats the whole person including body, emotions, mind and spirit creating many beneficial effects that include relaxation, feelings of peace and wellbeing. Many people have reported miraculous results. Getting great results from it is not dependent on our intellectual capacity or spiritual development and it is available to everyone.

Reiki is spiritual in nature but it is not a religion, there's no dogma and there is nothing we need to believe in order for it to work. It works whether we believe in it or not. Another reason I feel it is important is because it is a tangible feeling of a good strong energy moving through and around us. This puts us in touch with the experience of energy and power in our core rather than simply having an intellectual concept of it. These good sensations we can feel flowing through us when we receive Reiki are from the same source as our own sensations of power and inspiration.

It can give us a head start and it becomes a source of strength in our initial stages that can continue throughout our adventure if we need it. Furthermore there is companionship and encouragement from the person who is giving the Reiki that becomes a fantastic ally on the path of our adventure. We must be careful who we enrol on our team when we commit to our plan which we will talk more about later in the sections on other people in our lives. A Reiki master can become a key member of our team. It is similar to a sports therapist there for physiotherapy and support as we play on the field of our adventure.

It is easy to find a Reiki practitioner in your area by using a search engine online. You will find a natural health centre close to you or an independent practitioner. Go and interview a few if you can find them and talk to them about what you are doing and what you would like to achieve, you will then be able to work together to find the ideal routine. Settle with one you feel a resonance with and one you feel comfortable opening up to, it's important to feel safe and comfortable in their presence.

If this section has resonated with you I highly recommend acting on it. But if this is not for you then please respect your intuition, I am not suggesting that it is essential to everyone's journey.

When the Voices Hinder Progress

We are going to be bringing our adventure out to play in the section coming soon. To help us take action and maintain the feeling of happiness we are generating from the Feel Good Game we are going to look at some further techniques. We have already talked about our adventure and the mind and we are now going to look into this in a bit more detail by discussing the voices *we all* experience in our own minds that can be a little challenging. Some voices are part of the mind chatter that can be responsible for making us feel unhappy and stop us from taking action. "I'm not good enough" is a perfect example. So we are going to look into what we can do about these. It helps to bring a smile with us into this section because the voices in our heads often lead to us taking ourselves way too seriously.

When I refer to voices I mean unhelpful things other people may have said to us that we keep repeating to ourselves or our own voice that keeps stating difficult and unhelpful comments. This is part of the chatter of the mind that is simply triggered by something but this time it has a little more emotional charge to it. Some voices like to frighten the life out of us when we first wake up. That moment at 5am when are still half asleep but part of us is wide awake. We would like to go back to sleep but the voices get really noisy. It's as if they know that we are half asleep and defenceless. The voices like to go on and on and they know how to get straight to our core. When we are convinced a negative voice is right about us, we believe in it, we get angry and conclude we are broken. These little gremlins can really start to disrupt progress if left unchecked. Perhaps this will start to happen when you finish reading this book. You will be really motivated and excited for a short period and then the voices will start to kick in. "Being happy just isn't for you, you aren't good at anything. Just get on with your life as it is..."

What we are going to learn here is that as soon as these types of negative voices begin we act to either stop or process them. There is a difference between a voice that comes with a strong feeling that we need to take a particular course of action and one that is simply based in paranoia. Playing the Feel Good Game Is an excellent way to identify the voices that are simply negative and fear based because we are much more aware of anything that makes us feel victimised or belittled. An intuitive voice does not victimise or belittle us and we must do something with ones that make us feel this way, otherwise they will drain us and bring us to a standstill.

When we begin something as important to us as our adventure it might trigger self judgement and criticism, the ego can really take hold. All sorts of stories and voices can emerge, by calming these down we can hear what is really going on inside and we can keep confidence in ourselves and our adventure high. We could speculate for years on where these voices come from. Maybe they come from our upbringing, our schooling or things that have happened to us. In an effort to eradicate negative voices I have helped myself and others recreate difficult scenarios under careful supervision within special environments to retrain the sub conscious. This has certainly helped in some circumstances but there is a simple observation that has arisen from my experience of working with my own and other people's voices. We all have the power to fuel them with further thinking or we have the power to stop them in their tracks.

The Constant Process of Thought & Analysis

Once upon a time there was a huge ball of love consciousness that was unbounded by space and time. It was bigger than anything we can imagine because it didn't have an end to it, it was simply just there and always had been. It was always in eternal bliss but there was a problem, it didn't have consciousness of itself. In other words it didn't have the ability we have to delve into a miniscule aspect of any part of itself or the world around it and form an opinion. So it decided to burst out of itself into what was called a 'cosmic day'. It used the stuff it was made of, which was its own consciousness and made it all vibrate at different frequencies which made things material. To create consciousness of itself it meant creating polarities such as day and night, light and dark, good and bad, here and there, near and far and because it was a day it had time.

With these clever things in place it meant that now there was a contrast between two complete opposites. This gave it a new perspective with consciousness of itself. None of it really existed and everything in it had no idea what it *really* was. It was all safe because it was made from love and actually it was all happening in one giant moment or now. In fact the now wasn't really there either, because the huge ball of love consciousness had always been there and always will be. It had just created something incredible so it could feel itself.

I was once told this story by one of my teachers when I was frustrated with myself for constantly generating thought and voices. It helped me to realise that we are part of a bigger process and the consciousness we have inside of ourselves is also constantly gaining experience through our senses. If it resonates with you then the story may help to put these 'voices' we have in our heads into a little context. The watcher we have inside of ourselves is assessing everything and continuously putting meaning on everything, it has been doing it since we were born and it will keep doing it until we die. It is phenomenal when we really stop to think about it but it is also a naturally occurring process *that just happens*. So of course we are going to develop voices! Blaming ourselves for the voices we have made up is pretty pointless and turning this powerful consciousness on ourselves to make judgement when these voices arise is not very helpful.

So instead can we begin to become aware of our own loving watcher behind the watcher? This is one of the reasons that we practise meditation, so we can quieten the constant process of thought and analysis. Since the mind is making meanings all the time in a constant process that is simply just happening we don't need to believe everything it stumbles upon! In other words the voices that tell us we are not good enough, quick enough, good looking enough or thin enough are deductions we made about ourselves when the watcher experienced something and then decided that this must be the truth. When we learn to feel the watcher watching all this we can learn to smile and perhaps giggle a bit then blatantly laugh at the ridiculousness that we have decided is a fact.

Consciousness will pick up any thought, concept or sensual experience and merge in to see and feel what's there, that's what it was designed to do. But as the experience is coming through us it has our flavour and the uniqueness of all of our own personal experience as a way of forming judgement and conclusions. But we don't have to take all that personally! Perhaps we are just a tiny part of something much bigger and very powerful, perhaps the watcher behind the watcher *is* the all powerful part.

Either way we couldn't have controlled these reactions as a child. We couldn't have stopped them forming into voices and judgements about ourselves. But do we have to believe them all now? I can remember asking my Mum as a child about a road sign close to our house that said "Blind people crossing". I finally asked her if that was for the blind people driving out of the blind people's home. I had thought that every time we had passed it for years as I was growing up! We wouldn't dream of continuing to believe in concepts about the world we decided were true as a child, so why should we do the same with ones we have made up about ourselves? My Mum did well not to laugh and reassured me that blind people tend not to drive.

So voices and thoughts are all they are, they are not a law that governs us. We can let go of the grip that negative or unhelpful voices have on us, we can acknowledge them for what they are with sincerity but we do not have to allow them to define us. If we agree with them and feed them with further thought they will limit us, stop us from being ourselves and stop us from living our adventure. Sometimes these negative voices are based on opinions we have heard from other people. When we are children we cannot help misinterpret what other people say about us sometimes but we often decide to take that information to define who we are. This can become a voice we are still carrying 30, 40 or 50 years later, I'm not so sure we should still be listening to these and taking them seriously if they are causing us pain and limiting our potential. We can begin to see them as old programs we have running in our hard drive that are not serving us. The more we learn to let go of these voices the less power we give them and the quicker the grip begins to loosen.

So coming next is a little exercise we can practise when an unwanted negative thought pattern begins to emerge. Remember stopping thought patterns is not the same as repressing emotion. We simply do not need to entertain negative thoughts for a second longer than necessary. We can acknowledge any new information but as soon as we intuitively know the mind has begun associating along a negative path, we stop. Or indeed if we find ourselves listening to a derogatory voice that is causing us to fear, doubt and judge then again we stop fuelling it. Imagine them a bit like unwanted fire, the sooner we do something about it the easier it is to handle.

For Use When the Voices Are Niggling & Distracting

Stop wherever you are and **feel your feet on the ground**

Ask yourself:

- Is this train of thought supporting my growth and my journey?
- Are these thoughts in line with what I value about myself and the world?
- From who's opinion is this train of thought **actually** true?
- Will I be better off if I just let this go?

Then...

- Smile at the thoughts and relax your body
- Focus on the feeling of your feet on the ground
- Allow the thoughts and any associated feelings to drain down.
  (As though you were opening a trap door in your neck that allowed it all to flush down into the ground).

If this sounds a bit strange or even too simple don't worry, give it a try. Remember how powerful our minds are and that we have the ability to stop negative voices and thoughts. The exercise above is firstly questioning the line of thought which helps us to break the spell. By smiling and relaxing we are engaging our truth back into the picture again. Then by focussing on the sensation of our feet on the ground we are bringing ourselves into the body and back into the moment. This stops the fanning of the fire.

Try it and practise it. Once we understand the concept we can work with our own inspiration and adapt these techniques into ways that might make them more bespoke for us. All we are doing is questioning the validity of the voices and stopping them by bringing ourselves back into the moment using our bodies. So you may choose to alter the wording slightly to suit you better.

I am under no illusions however that this is going to make a difference in all circumstances. Don't worry there is more to come for when we are in utter crisis and just want to collapse in a heap of despair!

To help us continue let's stay with the idea of this amazing consciousness probe we have that feels and experiences everything. It will be this that helps us to process the difficult feelings and states that the voices can create in us. We are going to look at a couple more techniques that will help us to do this. Remember the purpose of all this is to bring us back to our centre of feel good, when we feel good we are in alignment, we are Finding Heart and we can continue with living our adventure.

To see how effective this consciousness probe is that we all have installed in us we are going to try an experiment. This will also help us to see where it is and what it is. But before we do that here is a little more on where these techniques are coming from. Through rigorously searching for and trying out any and every personal development technique I have come across for the past twenty years in relation to authentic living, it has come as a wonderful realisation that all of the gurus and teachers around the world that use effective and powerful techniques are all really teaching very similar concepts.

They all have variations on them and different styles of teaching them but I feel confident in saying that either they are stemming from the ancient techniques that get downloaded into the enlightened masters we have all heard of or they are getting downloaded again through the current masters of our time. By the term downloaded I mean something that is coming through us when we have a moment of insight through a clear channel we have stumbled upon inside us or one we have formed through years of practise.

In my experience we are all connected and I know this sounds a bit spiritual until we have personal experience of such matters but to me there seems to be a universal consciousness and we are all tapped into it. Our bodies have natural abilities to heal themselves when we fall over and cut ourselves and in my experience we have natural abilities to heal ourselves spiritually and emotionally. If we all sit quietly for long enough we all tend to reach similar conclusions about the most effective ways to heal, which is a beautiful and very reassuring thing.

So all the techniques in this book are ones that are widely known about and some for thousands of years and during the countless hours I have been meditating myself over the last 15 or so years I have thoroughly practised these techniques. The ones you will find here are the techniques I have found to be the most effective and the easiest to learn. What we are interested in as Finding Heart adventurers is how we can use these techniques to move us forward with our dreams to live our own lives in love, purpose and forgiveness because let's be honest is there anything better?

Practising this next one will give us direct experience of our own innate ability to shift difficult feeling and we can use it to bring us back to our centre of feel good.

The Consciousness Probe

Find a feeling in the body that is prominent. If you are experiencing pain or discomfort anywhere it's perfect for this, although any feeling at all will work. We are going to send our probe or awareness into the core of the feeling.

- *Sit quietly somewhere, put your notepad and pen down next to you. Take a deep breath and close your eyes.*
- *If it is an uncomfortable feeling we already know it hurts and we don't like it, let go of that for a moment.*
- *The trick here is to get objective about the feeling.*

The following questions are simply an exercise to introduce us to the healing probe we have within us, I know they sound silly but the good news is there is no wrong answer to them. The questions are simply engaging the probe. The more detailed our answers are the better it will work.
Take a moment to close your eyes and focus all your awareness into the feeling or pain. Simply stay with it for a few minutes and explore it.

Take your notebook and just write down the answers to the following questions about the pain or feeling you are witnessing.

1. *If the pain or feeling had a shape what shape would it be? It might be any shape at all from a thin wavy sheet to a round blob or it might be perfectly symmetrical.*

2. *If the pain or feeling had a size how long would it be in centimetres or inches?*
3. *If the pain or feeling had a width how long would it be in centimetres or inches?*
4. *If the pain or feeling were to have a depth what would that be in centimetres or inches?*
5. *If the pain or feeling had a colour what colour would it be?*
6. *Has the pain or feeling moved or can you feel it moving?*

Have you got a list of answers to the questions above?

What has happened to the feeling? If it's changed somehow that's perfect. Have another go at the questions to see if the answers are different. You will find that if you delve more and more into the feeling and keep answering the questions the feeling will disperse and disappear.

Has the pain gone? Well don't look now but you've just witnessed the self healing power of your own consciousnesses

Well done. Next time you have a headache try this, you will be amazed. Don't forget you can make someone else's pain go away by taking them through this exercise as well. It will of course help them and also further your experience.

So now we come to the main technique that all this has been leading up to and one that I strongly advise you get into the habit of practising when the voices and the feelings become overwhelming. This is the one to use when nothing else has worked and the thoughts and feeling have taken over. It is great when you find you have reacted strongly to something that has happened or if you have over reacted to something that someone has said to you. It could be the time when you feel most upset and want to cry. Part of the reason crying is so relieving is because it brings us down into our bodies and releases energy, which is what we are going to do here. But this time we are going to benefit from the energy as well as letting it out.

Some of the voices we have in our heads are our triggers that have the power to really upset us. We all have triggers and all that means is that we have a voice in us that we have given power and meaning to. What the voice is saying may not be true but some have the ability to pull us far away from our centre *because* of the power we have given it. The people closest to us usually have the best fingers in their pockets to pull these triggers or push these buttons in us. It's partly why we chose them because these nuggets of energy need acknowledging and *reclaiming* into consciousness and we can use our probe for this. These are the voices we need to take a little time to work with...

So if we are in overwhelm and really struggling we must stop and give ourselves time to remedy it. The best way to learn this technique is to treat it like a short meditation. Mentioning the word meditation could cause some rolling of the eyes, perhaps because it is quite an elusive art and it's hard to tell if anything is happening when it is practised. Also no-one likes sitting still in silence for too long because it gets so noisy and frustrating listening to the incessant chatter in the mind. I certainly went through all of this during my study. When I sat my first silent retreat at a mediation centre in my hometown of Brighton in the UK I expected a serious explosion of enlightenment by about day five. I asked myself how much longer can I possibly be expected to do this before I am welcomed into the club by Buddha himself. It's a little more subtle I discovered but through letting go of expectation and judgement we can use the environment of meditation to learn how to disperse these difficult feelings in a much shorter period of time. Once you have practised this technique a couple of times you will soon be able to process yourself whilst standing in a supermarket waiting for your turn at the checkout.

I taught a version of this next technique to my grandmother to help her to process the anxiety she used to experience through living by herself. She had no idea what meditation was and yet she found the technique to work wonders. Under a thin veil of noise we can find there is a very wise and peaceful version of us all waiting to help. This next technique will take a few minutes or longer if you need it to be. During this time the mind will wander and we are not expecting our thoughts to stop. I asked one of the teachers on my retreat how I could stop thoughts arising in my mind because it was disturbing my practise. He smiled and replied 'Grass grows on the ground, hair grows on our heads and thoughts arise in our minds. You can't stop it from happening.' Don't worry; we simply acknowledge we have wandered and return to the technique. No judgement.

Go somewhere you won't be disturbed. It is OK to tell someone you need a few minutes and you will be back if you are in overwhelm with difficult thoughts and feelings. Even if you are boiling over with emotions it is still the perfect time to do this. Don't worry if initially the feelings intensify or if you begin to cry, just let it come. Don't worry if the phrases in the technique sound a bit strange to you they are to help your body release the energy that is overwhelming you. When we start to distract the mind the suffering associated will begin to subside; trust that your body will know what to do. Remember, into the feeling is the best way through and the stronger it is the more power you will be reclaiming.

The Clearing & Reclaiming Technique

Sit comfortably with your back straight; with your hands in your lap and your feet flat on the floor. Or if you like to sit cross legged with your hands in your lap, this is just as good.

We need to come down into the body so close your eyes and take a couple of deep breaths. Allow yourself to relax and let go with each out-breath.

Imagine the crown of your head is being held up by a cord. Keep you back straight, tilt your head forward slightly and let everything relax and drop away from the cord.

Now breathe into your belly and *feel it* expand and *feel it* contract as you breathe out. This will be your reference point, keep your awareness on the feeling of your belly and chest expanding and contracting.

Each time you notice the mind has wandered bring your awareness back to the feeling of the air coming in and out of your body.

Keep doing this for at least a couple of minutes. It is OK that the mind may be fizzing with thoughts; the aim right now is to bring your attention away from your thoughts and into the feelings in your body. This is the way to relief.

Now turn to the place in your body that is holding all the tension and re-run the scenario in your mind that caused the anger, sadness or difficult feeling.

Settle your awareness on the associated feeling. Now begin to breathe in and out as though you are breathing air *through* that place inside your body. Exactly as you were breathing air into the chest and belly, simply imagine that you are now sucking and blowing air through that part of your body. Do this several times or until you are really focussed on the feeling.

Say to yourself:

"As I feel it, I allow myself to let go of *any* judgement I have about this feeling.

Pause and breathe. Then say the following to yourself.

'I feel the presence of myself in this moment'

'I now choose to reclaim the power of this feeling'.

'As I reclaim it I feel the power surging through my body'.

Feel the energy dispersing and returning back to you.

Keep your awareness focussed on the feeling and keep repeating the process as you need to.

When you are complete take your time to gently and gradually come back into the room. Begin to stretch and move your body and then slowly open your eyes.

Please don't leap up and march out the room, come round gently.

Hopefully the feeling you were working with will have dispersed and energised you in the process. Even if this has happened to a small extent then that is fantastic, the more we learn to lessen our grip and allow the body to process the feelings, the better.

The intention behind these techniques is for us to have something to turn to when we get really upset and so we can do something with the energy that is causing us the pain and discomfort. Rather than spending hours or days stewing over something we have reacted to our aim is to bring ourselves back to our centre so we can Find Heart again and continue working with our adventure.

Whatever happens please don't allow yourself to be blown around by painful thoughts and voices without applying something. In my experience analysing an uncomfortable voice or negative thought pattern in the hope of resolving it brings no end of torment. If it feels limiting and restrictive there is never *ever* any resolution from our own analysis of the thought itself, all we are doing is fuelling the fire and giving the voice more power.

Practise dropping this powerful consciousness probe or probe of awareness if you prefer into the body. When the probe is in our heads and we turn it on ourselves it is pointed and can easily prick something, when it is in our bodies it is round and soft and helps the body to heal and process.

When we have a breakdown, get really upset or really fall out with ourselves our greatest endeavour is to bring ourselves back on track and back to our centre without blame or judgement.

We can choose to break *ourselves* out of any destructive cycle of emotion, cycle of thought or self criticism using these techniques. Remember no-one else is going to come and save us, they all have their own journeys to walk. Our hearts and our happiness are always waiting to greet us again. Do what needs to be done to find them again.

The Heart of the Matter

- ♥ An intuitive voice does not victimise or belittle us and we must do something with ones that make us feel this way.
- ♥ Voices and thoughts are all they are, they are not a law that governs us.
- ♥ When we are in overwhelm and really struggling we must stop and give ourselves time to remedy it.
- ♥ Try not to allow yourself to be blown around by painful thoughts and voices without applying something.
- ♥ If it feels limiting and restrictive there is never *ever* any resolution from our own analysis of the thought itself, all we are doing is fuelling the fire and giving the voice more power.
- ♥ The more we learn to let go of these voices the less power we give them and the quicker the grip begins to loosen.
- ♥ By focussing on the sensation of our feet on the ground we bring ourselves into the body and back into the moment.
- ♥ Into a feeling is the best way through.
- ♥ When we have a breakdown, get really upset or really fall out with ourselves our greatest endeavour is to bring ourselves back on track and back to our centre without blame or judgement.
- ♥ Take a moment to add any observations or resistance you are feeling into your notebook.

The Sound Walk

The process of Clearing and Reclaiming is a great technique to process really difficult feelings that arise from thoughts and voices that have got the better of us. However sometimes we need something to get us out of the head and into the body that involves movement.

Drive or walk somewhere you will be relatively alone if possible, somewhere quiet and away from busy roads and streets, you are going to need to make noise without drawing attention to yourself. When you are walking along take five deep breaths in, on your sixth breath you are going to make a sound when you breathe out. This sound is the letter 'A' but phonetically it sounds like the letter 'R'.

So breathe in deeply and on your out-breath make a long 'ARR' sound for as long as you can and as loud as you feel comfortable. Louder is better if you can without attracting attention to yourself. If you have a difficult feeling inside focus your awareness there and feel the vibration of your voice running through it.

This vibration is helping to shift the thought pattern and also the feeling in the body; the walking is bringing us out of the thought centre and into the body. Depending on the severity of the instance that's caused the reaction I don't recommend screaming it out. There is some benefit to screaming a feeling out into a pillow or even screaming out anywhere when we are alone. However during my experience and research of this particular clearing technique our bodies can begin to learn that this is what we are going to do next. So our anger will escalate to warrant screaming. It may have some relief afterwards but it is agitating and not something we want to develop into a habit, unless of course our bodies need to do this in certain circumstances. Making the 'ARR' sound whilst walking may sound a bit lame compared to screaming but we are more interested in keeping our agitation to a minimum whilst giving our bodies a release.

If possible continue to walk for the duration of an hour in total and if you can go somewhere that has a distant horizon, keep your focus there as often as it feels comfortable. This is known to be very effective for helping to clear and align us and promote a feeling of well being again.

It's important to have a range of options for processing ourselves, always remember trying one of them is always better than nothing. One final note I will say is sometimes we may be feeling too exhausted and upset to do anything to make ourselves feel better. So if lying in bed to recuperate is what you really need to do then for goodness sake do it, *without judgement*!

III

Deep roots and happy shoots

Bringing Our Adventure out to Play!

It is time to bring out the adventure you have been working on from the commitment exercise earlier on in the book. We are going to be breaking it up into manageable sections that will enable us to begin to take action and make it a reality.

Bring what you have uncovered as you have worked through the sections you have read so far. Dare to be as honest as you can and highlight anything that has felt inconsistent with your truth. Does the *feeling* and motivation behind your choice feel right to you? Check in with yourself about any stories that you may be running. What do the thoughts and voices that you experience tell you about what you have chosen? Try to be as clear as you can about anything that is not coming from you.

Or anything that might be stopping you from choosing the thing you *really* want.

Trust that the good feelings you have been generating and the techniques you have learned to process yourself are helping you to find your truth. How has the work on your values affected your chosen adventure? Is your choice in line with your core beliefs about yourself and the world around you?

Use this coming space to begin an adventure that is bespoke to you, it can be our secret for the moment. Use it to uncover the course of action that is coming from your heart. The feelings in our bodies associated to our adventure should be feeling similar to that part of our lives when we felt in our flow and most happy; the time when we felt in alignment with our own values.

The coming adventure that we will bring into reality is not going to be one that we feel we 'should' be doing, or the one that was decided for us at school. It is your adventure. If it happens to coincide with what other people or establishments hoped for us then that is great if it is the truth. This choice is not about how much money you will be able to make or whether or not it is what other people expect of you, it is what you genuinely want for yourself. Money and admiration will be far more sustainable if this is *your* adventure.

Make the time you are investing into reading this book worthwhile. Find the heart to work with yourself as though you were working with a loved one. Would you let them take a course of action that you knew wasn't right for them? Think of the hard work and commitment they may be walking towards trusting your judgement and advice that they are doing the right thing. Give yourself the love that you deserve and be honest. It is far better to be honest and begin something new than it is to keep doing the same thing over and over expecting a different result.

To find the persistence and faith that we need to make something a success in our lives means it must be aligned with who we really are. Otherwise it will fall over when we need it most. If you are not sure then begin along the lines that feel right to you. For instance become the personal trainer to walk the path to realise that it is in fact a sport therapist that is calling you. Many paths involve a series of experiences to get us to where we need to be.

This is different to the voice in our heads that keeps telling us we 'should' walk a particular path. Begin to differentiate from what is in your heart and a voice that has come from somewhere else. Sometimes we crave the love and acceptance we think we will get if we follow the life path our parents or loved ones want for us. Is this affecting the choice you are making for yourself? What advice would you give a loved one in this instance? Would you advise them to follow the family footsteps so their parents can feel more comfortable discussing their daughter's or son's progress at a dinner party? Or would you encourage them to follow the path that truly makes them happy?

This is the type of enquiry I invite you to take with you as you now progress with this book. We may not get the course of action exactly right the first time but if we are aware of the obvious thoughts and voices that might be leading us astray the better the chance we are giving ourselves. Life is too short to walk blindly when it's perfectly possible to find the courage to open our eyes.

Take this journey to find the courage to be yourself, celebrate who you are and above all enjoy the journey. This is the best gift we can offer the world that will be around us along the way.

The Mind Map

In this section we are going to look at a technique that is tried and tested for brainstorming an idea and one that has bought many of my own adventures into reality. The time has come to put pen to paper and bring what is most important to us into this work space and onto the Finding Heart drawing-board.

We are going to get practical and begin breaking things down into manageable steps and courses of action. To do this we are going to create a mind map. Perhaps you have already begun your journey, you are already making steps and that is fantastic, if you haven't got a mind map for your adventure I invite you to try one.

A mind map is a piece of software or simply a drawing that we use to brainstorm our idea into workable sections, I have used these for my adventures throughout my adult life or at least since I have begun using a computer. If you have a tablet they are great for these maps or any computer is perfect.

Here is an example –

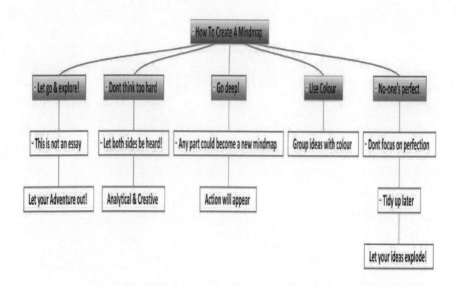

This is an excellent way to get a huge amount of information out of ourselves. A mind map as you can see is a way to brainstorm and by doing this we are doing several things:

- It unlocks the information we are storing in our brains by using a graphic technique.
- It makes use of all the cortical skills including spatial awareness, number, rhythm, logic, colour and of course word.
- We can roam about in our minds searching for useful data.
- It connects us up to our inspiration and gives us a platform to record insight.
- It is brilliant to refer to, set tasks and monitor progress and any category on a mind map can become a whole new map of its own.

It will also serve as an excellent way to help us to take key pieces of action that will bring the whole together. I'll explain in more detail how this works when we refer to the example coming soon.

Drawing them out is a lovely creative process and certainly the way to go if you like the idea of it. They work on a blackboard which allows more room to expand or a large sheet of paper that will stick on the wall. However be aware these maps grow and grow as you uncover new information on each category. When you go for it and start brainstorming they get very big very quickly which is why I personally do them on a computer or a tablet because you can zoom in and out and move it all around. I will share with you some examples of the software you can use to make them shortly.

Creating them on a screen is also fast. As soon as you think of the next thing you want to put down you just click a button and a new bubble appears. Each bubble has a particular name according to its position on the mind map which you will discover if you decide to go with an onscreen version. I suggest trying one on screen if you can and seeing how you get on, the mind works pretty fast and you may find it harder to keep up with your thoughts and ideas if you are drawing it, especially if you are excited and flowing from inspiration.

The other advantage of course is when we are out and about we can add to our mind map and refer to it as and when we need to. One word of caution you must back up any mind map you create! It's horrible losing a big map you have been working on for some time. If you create a map on a tablet for instance you can save them to a file online or you can email them to yourself.

I use Mind Genius and you will find a free Mind Genius app on your tablet which you can use to your heart's content. As I say you can back them up or email them to yourself but you will only be able to open them on your PC if you have installed Mind Genius. You can start a free trial at www.mindgenius.com. Another version of this software is 'Freeplane' which is free and you can find it online to get all the details you need to use it.

So what exactly are we doing here? We are beginning to bring our adventure from our hearts out into the world to make it a reality. In my experience it just isn't healthy to have an adventure in our hearts that we are really excited about that keeps turning from heart to mind and mind to heart. It needs to get out! The very creative process of bringing something into manifest is what makes being human so incredibly fulfilling and the longer we keep something so important cooped up inside of ourselves the more damage it does as it keeps bumping around inside of us. It has been my observation from working with people to help them bring their adventures into their lives that they become completely different people when they have finally begun to take action and begin living it. Before they are awash with ideas, judgements, preconceptions and repressed energy. Once the commitment begins there is flow, release, direction and they can't remember what all the fuss was about.

We cannot truly know our adventure until we bring it forth to the stage of life. This is where the adventure begins and the environment of kindness and compassion awakens. Our minds may be able to visualise new worlds but we have to pass this vision through the mechanics of our body and speech to bring it forth. We are incredible creatures but we are also organic beings doing our best. Let go of the fear of making mistakes, mistakes are how we learn and discover what does and doesn't work. We are no different to a potter and the clay. The potter can see the pot in his or her mind, the perfect environment is set and the best tools are ready. Who can know exactly what pot will come into reality and wouldn't it be boring if we did? Enjoy the process and be patient with the potter but if weeks are wasted circling the wheel, contemplating the idea, changing the mind from pot to bowl and never beginning, the potter may start to feel unwell. Wouldn't you agree?

Our mind maps will become a tool we can use to begin to transfer our adventure from our heart and mind into the outside world. It is a half way medium between heart and reality and it will become a building block for the process.

What is the best environment we can create for ourselves? Let's establish a Head Quarters to undergo this creative process. This will be the space we can use at home or maybe at work that can become the hub for our adventure. But just before we do that...

A Friendly Warning.

In my experience I have found I can run a source of income as well as my adventure if I need it. In other words I am only focussing on one adventure but I am also maintaining another venture or job that is feeding me and paying the bills. Now in some cases our adventure will become our source of income and a quick word on this if this is the plan. It is super tempting to leave our job so the focus becomes 100% onto the adventure that will provide an income. But this quickly becomes pretty hair raising. It is possible to do this of course and many have but it wouldn't be very fair of me if I didn't mention some factors that can become scary monsters when doing this. For example if the adventure is to start a business and there is already personal evidence that the idea produces money it can seem safe to assume it will produce a reasonable income quickly. Here are some considerations –

- *A few sales or customers initially can easily be luck and the market you are depending on can change or disappear overnight if you don't have the resources and experience to change with it.*
- *Businesses are expensive to operate (it's cheaper if it is online but we still need to proceed with caution).*
- *Any debt accumulated to live on can be very difficult to catch up to and pay off again.*
- *The psychological pressure of making our adventure our source of income too early can change the feeling of it and if not calculated carefully it can soon become a heavy weight to burden (Of course if this adventure is truly aligned with our values & passion we will do*

whatever it takes but how much pressure do we want to withstand initially?)

- *Making a passion into a money-making venture changes its nature; we can only witness how this feels once we have done it, so we need to be in a strong place if it is not what we are expecting.*

Thank you for listening. I know you know what you are doing.

Establishing our HQ

Our bedroom is OK but the energy can be a bit conflicting in terms of sleep space vs. work space. If there is another room in the house we can use for our project that won't be disturbed by others then this is ideal, but if the bedroom is the only option then go with it 100%. We will need files for paper that we accumulate, we will need dedicated files on a computer that can't be accidently affected by another and ideally we need to find the space as we left it when we come back to it. This doesn't mean it turns into a mess that will frustrate other members of the house hold. The idea is that this space becomes the studio for our creation and there is a saying that says, "Order promotes organic growth".

In this space it is great if we can use a wall to put pictures and material for ease and direct viewing. Either directly on the wall if we are not going to damage it (or we have the skills to repair it) or onto a large pin board. These details are really down to personal preference of course and how we work as individuals. In my experience I have found if everything disappears into files on a computer things can become a bit illusive whereas if I have images and progress physically in front of me it helps. We are also gradually creating a vision board which can include images of where we are going and hoping to achieve. All this is bringing what is within us, out, so we can meet it, process it and act on it.

Action

We could go into the tiniest detail of how we actually bring our ideas and adventures into reality but my belief and hope is that once we have addressed the fears and pitfalls that stop us from taking action we will find our flow and the bespoke way in which it all works well for us as an individual. So once we have created our HQ and started brainstorming our idea onto a mind map let's look at how this can begin to translate into action.

The next mind map you will find coming up is one I have created on a tablet using the free Mind Genius app. It is a re-creation of the mind map I drew when I started an adventure renovating real estate for rental and resale a few years back. You'll be pleased to know this business was a great success but it took faith, persistence and commitment to make it a reality. It was inspired from my passion for carpentry and building work that I had learned with my Grandfather who was in a similar business when he was alive. It was also in alignment with my passion for working with people, as we know for an adventure to be sustainable it must be in alignment with our values. So this is a good example to show you.

Before we look at the example of the map coming up it is important to note this is just an example I have made to illustrate a method of translating thought and idea into action. I'll explain what I mean by that in a moment. A real mind map, as you will experience, may be much bigger but if I make it too big and complicated it won't be clear for our purposes here. However what I have created below are real factors I needed to take into consideration. I was also starting out with very little of my own money so I needed to get creative to make it work.

You can see I have started with the main category which is 'Buy House'. The other branches coming off this are then aspects of buying a property I was going to need to consider. They include the money I would need to find, where the property will be, what team I will need in place to help me and then you will notice one of the categories is 'How will I find the property?'

You can see there is an orange box around 'Find local investors'. This is an example of how relevant actions we need to take come about from creating a mind map. The real map I drew went into further detail on the categories above and there were more categories as well, I am just reiterating this so you don't get the impression that this is as big as they get. You will find all this out with your own maps and the size of them as they come through you.

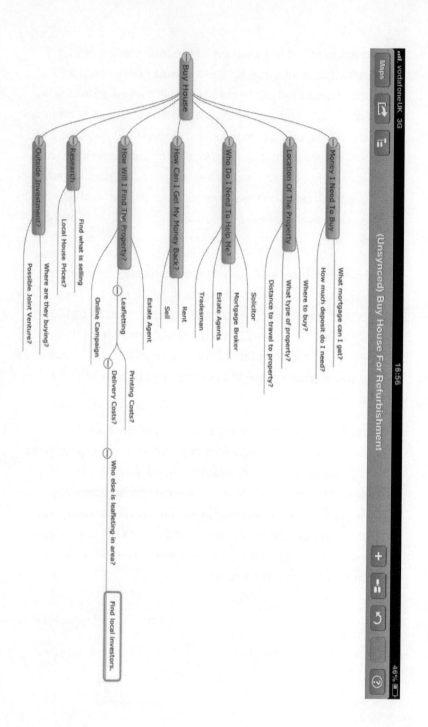

What I would like to show you here with this example is that you can see how the categories we create lead to questions that we can no longer answer by ourselves. This means we need to get out there and begin researching, networking, meeting people who work in the particular field we are interested in and start asking questions. Indeed much of the information we need might be found online and we can get pretty far just by making phone calls. Whatever needs to be done, this is how a mind map leads to action and in other words we can only go so far before we need to gather information that gives us the key to the next part of our adventure. Before we know it we are out there making it happen.

Reality takes on a whole new perspective when we begin exploring what we do and don't know on our mind map which often leads to finding people who *are already doing what we want to do*. Not only do we see that what we want to do is entirely possible (which gives us confidence) it also shows us what we need to do next. Step by step we gradually meet the right people who may even want to work with us and often put money into the business. This was my experience in the example above and typical of how new ventures get off the ground.

It doesn't matter that the particular example here is a property purchase that lead to a business, what is important is that we can see the example of how the skills and techniques we are learning in this book mixed with carefully thought through courses of action will lead to our adventure becoming a reality for us. The man who started his fish restaurant would have gone through the process of thought to research to action. A plan to travel the world will happen with the same format as would any other type of venture, passion or idea in whatever context it is. All we are doing here is breaking the process down into a format that we can follow. One that works for us as a unique individual and one that we can learn to protect from the sabotage that can come from inside and outside of us.

So How Would *You* Do This?

Once we reveal a course of action it's important in my experience to get organised. The course of action can be anything from researching a particular category on line, it might mean making a particular phone call or it may indeed mean leaving the house and going to meet someone. Each of these actions asks us to be prepared and organised. We also need to make sure we are actually going to do it. For instance if we put a day in our diary and commit to making it happen by this time we will be moving forwards step by step. Any organisation must be done in line with how we as individuals work best. Ask yourself how you work best. What do you need in your calendar to help you complete tasks? What may work for someone else may not work for you or me. So getting organised has to be in alignment with our values and our feelings.

This goes for everything we are learning here, everything must be taken and applied in a way that becomes bespoke to us, this is all part of Finding Heart. We can find heart in how we do everything. But we also have to get things done if we are to move forwards. So we keep asking ourselves the question "How would *I* do this?" When we uncover a piece of action that needs taking we need to ask ourselves what the most effective way to do it will be that will get us the most effective results.

So we ask ourselves what is the best way to set tasks, and then we enquire as to the best way to get the most from the piece of action we need to take. In my case if I need to make a phone call I like to prepare all the questions I will need to ask. It's also important to retain all the information we uncover; to process it into documents we can keep or store or keep on our computer. Gradually we are getting into the habit of taking our adventure seriously and honouring each step of the way.

If something doesn't work then we try a different way and we never assume that just because something works well for someone else that it will work for us. Step by step we are walking our adventure on a daily basis and we should be trying to do at *least* one thing towards the becoming of our adventure every day. Even if we are at a family gathering for the weekend we can still check our mind map and schedule once during the day when we are in the bathroom! It is the commitment to our adventure that will make it materialise and by making our commitment bespoke to how we know we like to do things, it will help to sustain it.

Keep making baby steps and there will be progress. Be brave and trust that when you leap the net will appear. If you are really feeling stuck about what adventure you should choose or you need support please contact me for a free consultation using the details provided at the end of the book. It would be my great pleasure to assist you.

The next coming sections are all about keeping our adventure safe and making sure it is nurtured in its early stages. So keep moving forwards, keep taking action and trust you are exactly where you should be.

Making Decisions

Before we move on we are going to look a technique to help us listen to our hearts and make the decisions we need to as we progress our adventure. It is useful for when we are really stuck and can't make a decision.

Let's take an example to use for the purposes of this exercise. I was working with somebody recently who was soon to be moving house. There were two options for a moving date, there were a few factors involved and he needed to work out the best time to move. The option of moving in earlier involved having to move during the week and getting settled more quickly. The other option was to move in at the end of the month. If he moved in at the end of the month there would be a period during which his family would be helping to provide somewhere for him to stay. Both options had things he needed to consider.

If he moved in during the week it may be a bit stressful due to work and he may not have time to settle in straight away and feel relaxed. However not having to move via his family could be a better solution. There were also some new pieces of furniture he needed to acquire and when would he do this? What will make the move as easy as possible? He also needed to think about packing and deciding what he will keep and what will be given away. There was a fair bit of stuff to sort through. It needed planning properly but first he needed to commit to the moving date because other people were involved in that part. So what was he going to do? This decision needed some attention.

I invited him to take the time to be quiet and still the mind which was shouting all sorts at him. I suggested the mind is fickle, it's only processing things and there is a process he could try to give it the correct information to process. Taking time to be sure is everyone's right. Unless we have to make a decision very quickly then that is different. When this is required of us, 9 times out of 10 it is our first feeling that is our heart, our instinctual response. Our feelings are our guidance system.

In this particular event there are various factors and so by using silence and the intelligence of the body it will be possible to hear its message and what will be the right course of action to take.

This process takes a few minutes and again during this time the mind will wander but remember: Grass grows on the ground, hair grows on our heads and thoughts arise in our mind; it just happens. We simply return to the technique we are practising when we are aware we have wandered, that is all we need to do. No judgement.

Finding Heart To Make a Decision

Find some quiet switch any phones to silent but keep one with you to use as a timer, which should be a gentle sound when it goes off.

Replicate the sitting position we used for the process of 'Clearing and Reclaiming'. Whichever way you choose to sit, try to sit in the same way each time. The mind and body will remember what it's about to do and begin to relax again.

- Close your eyes.
- Breathe in fully and then say 'one' to yourself as you breathe out steadily and fully.
- Allow your body to relax on the out-breath.
- Repeat the process saying 'two' on your out-breath and repeat until you reach ten.
- Come round gently.

Hopefully this will have distracted the mind and you feel a little more still. If you are still feeling a bit frantic repeat the breathing exercise again. When you are ready start your timer to countdown ten minutes and close your eyes again. Or try 5 minutes if you prefer.

- Speak the two options of your decision and then let it go.
- Do this by finding a prominent sensation in the lower part of your body to focus your awareness. Or use the feeling of sitting you can feel in your legs.
- Close your eyes and try to keep them relaxed in there as you focus on the sensation.

- Keep bringing the attention back to the sensation you have chosen when the mind wanders.
- When the timer goes off gently open your eyes. When you are ready and switch it off and remain sitting as you are.

Now close your eyes again and place your left hand on your chest. Then say the first choice to yourself.

So in this case it will be, 'I am moving into the flat during the week in February'. Then notice the sensation in the body.

Then say the second choice, 'I am moving into the flat on the weekend at the beginning of March.' Then again notice the sensation in the body.

You will notice that the feelings are different. One of the feelings will rise and the other will be a sensation that is falling. Go with the feeling that rises, you will also notice it feels better. This is your body inspiration and learning to trust it helps it to become more and more accessible.

The Heart of the Matter

- ♥ Reiki is a great fuel for adventures. It is excellent for strength and clarity.
- ♥ The feelings in our bodies associated to our adventure should be feeling similar to that part of our lives when we felt in our flow and most happy.
- ♥ It is far better to be honest and begin something new than it is to keep doing the same thing over and over expecting a different result.
- ♥ To find the persistence and faith that we need to make something a success in our lives means it must be aligned with who we really are.
- ♥ Begin to differentiate from what is in your heart and a voice that has come from somewhere else.
- ♥ Sometimes we crave the love and acceptance we think we will get if we follow the life path our parents or loved ones want for us.
- ♥ A mind maps is a tool we can use to begin to transfer our adventure from our heart and mind into the outside world.
- ♥ We cannot truly know our adventure until we bring it forth to the stage of life.
- ♥ Reality takes on a whole new perspective when we begin exploring what we do and don't know on our mind map.
- ♥ Let go of the fear of making mistakes, mistakes are how we learn and discover what does and doesn't work.

- The psychological pressure of making our adventure our source of income too early can soon become a heavy weight to burden.
- Any organisation must be done in line with how we as individuals work best. Ask yourself how you work best.
- We should be trying to do at *least* one thing towards the becoming of our adventure every day.
- Taking time to be sure is everyone's right.
- Consider the location of HQ well and take the time to make it just right.
- Add any observations or resistance you are feeling into your notebook ☺

Our Adventure and Other People in Our Lives

"The person who says it cannot be done should not interrupt the person doing it" Chinese proverb

We come now to look at the art of Finding Heart with the friends, family and loved ones in our lives. Listening to our *own* hearts does not mean losing people around us. But if we are going to commit we are going to have to change things in our lives that no longer serve us. There may well be a backlash from the people around us if we choose to make changes and begin doing what we really want to do. We now take on the mantra *'How do I feel? What do I want?'* This is how we can cut through what is old reaction to circumstance and what is actually our truth. When we learn to listen to our truth more effectively then we are gradually becoming more and more in line with our flow. When we are living in our own flow the easier life becomes.

We have people in our lives that spread across a wide range of type of personalities. We might have some who are happy with their jobs, their lifestyles and their routines. They might go out each weekend, party and then get back to their weekly lives as normal on a Monday. Perhaps they have the odd holiday here and there but mainly nothing changes year to year.

Are there some that will understand when we are going through a change or starting a new idea or project and some that might not? Do some still need us to come out in the evenings for a drink or to meet them at the weekend? Is that still going to serve us? Perhaps it does or perhaps we need more time to focus, think and prepare especially if we have a full time job as well as our new venture.

If there are big party people in our lives are we going to *need* to keep clear of them for a while? What if they don't want us to change? How are we going to deal with that without upsetting ourselves or them? What if we are beginning to think about finding the set of people that are either in full support of what we are doing or have direct experience of what we are seeking. This is what we shall be looking at here.

Who Do We Talk to About Our Adventure?

Firstly here is a guideline that might trigger a bit of a reaction but from my own experience of working with myself and others we have to consider the importance of this because of the risk of what can happen when it is ignored.

Avoid talking to or asking advice from a friend or family member about a new idea, a new venture, or anything that you are personally designing in the very early stages *unless* they have direct experience of working with what you are about to do.

What I mean by direct experience is if they work or have worked in the same industry as your idea or project or have actually done what you are about to do themselves.

In my experience of talking to people who are finding the courage to initiate a change, countless excellent ideas and projects struggle unnecessarily or go by the wayside because they have been shared with someone who doesn't know what they are talking about. When you have a new idea think of it as a tiny little green shoot, like the ones you get when you plant Cress as a child. Imagine one of those little plants by itself and how delicate it is. Talking to friends and family members about a new idea is like putting the vulnerable little plant on a motorway. There is every chance it might get obliterated. I want to put this image in your mind to help embed this piece of advice.

Friends and family members mean well, they don't mean to put us off but 99% of the time they will say something that can crush our inspiration and our plans. They will have lots to say about our idea, oh yes! They will suddenly know all about it and they might relate it to other things we have tried in the past. The risky part is we love them and we respect their judgement and opinion which is why we go to them in the first place. Remember we may only take their opinion seriously because they are a friend or family member; they have great influence over us and we are very likely looking for approval from them. But the effect they can have on us emotionally and psychologically can very easily lead to a simple outcome:

SPLAT! And the little plant is gone or at best pretty damaged. They didn't mean to, like the car on the motorway. It didn't mean to hit the little plant; it probably didn't even see it.

You're little plant might make it to the other side of the motorway unharmed but who wants to take that risk?

Unless somebody has *personal* experience of working in the same industry as our idea or concept, don't ask their advice or opinion. It is not only a waste of time but very dangerous for an idea. It is hard to know whether what they have said is true or not and this is because the idea is just an idea, it is vulnerable and needs looking after. When we speak to someone who has personal experience of what we are dealing with they will give us advice we can use. But still we must be careful. Do we really need to talk to anyone at this stage? We can find out all sorts of information on any topic from the internet. If we are about to design a new product or service and need to speak to someone we can speak initially to someone who deals with new inventors and designers, such as a patent officer or an intellectual property solicitor or advisor. Choose experienced people who are used to talking to people who have new ideas and they will take you seriously.

Of course it's perfectly possible that our new idea may not be viable in the way we see it for one reason or another but we need to find this out for ourselves using the correct resources and *we* need to be satisfied that this is the case. Consider carefully who we take advice from and who we spend time with when we are preparing for something or bringing a new concept into the world.

So how has all that settled with you? Does it sound a bit harsh? It is only through experience of working with myself and with other people's adventures that I bring this to our attention. I am not suggesting for one moment that we cannot have the support and counsel of our own friends and family for our adventure once it is a reality, I am only suggesting that in its early stages we must be careful who we turn to for advice.

If our adventure is based in the need for approval we must gently acknowledge that fact and consider again if what we are looking to achieve is definitely coming from our own hearts. When our adventure is truly born from our own inspiration and strength of heart trust that we don't need anyone to tell us we are doing the right thing, we already know. We set about making it happen and if this happens to generate much approval and praise then that is simply a delightful cause and effect.

The possible need for approval here is a good example of where the book is simply bringing this type of awareness onto our radar to give us the opportunity to make particular distinctions for ourselves within the message itself.

Ok onto the next bit

Forgiveness

"Forgiveness is giving up hope of a better yesterday".

What does forgiveness have to do with our adventure? Forgiveness is incredibly powerful and very healing. In my experience absolutely anything we are holding onto from the past is blocking us from the possibilities of the future. It's another pair of glasses we are wearing that makes everything look tainted by an experience we have had that we are clinging onto because either we refuse to forgive someone else or ourselves. The old becomes an anchor we religiously cling to so we can be right about something and then we get confused about what we are doing. If we were to let go of something it might mean to us that we are saying that what happened was OK and we are condoning it. So we cling on maintaining that the tighter the grip the more we are telling the person off for getting something terribly wrong and really hurting us. Or are we simply doing that to ourselves? Have a look at this if it is ringing true, be gentle. Anything painful we are holding onto from the past is like a dark space in our sphere void of love and understanding. Those spaces are 'forgiving' love and understanding back to again.

Any act of anger, hate or a grave mistake that we have been witness to has stemmed from a place of error, ignorance, hurt or a program running in someone else. It is not their true nature if we can allow ourselves to believe that we all stem from love. From here we can apply forgiveness and understanding into anything we or anyone else has done. Or we can go on feeding the block that is only limiting and affecting us.

People mean well, mostly all of us do. But we are just human and we can be very unreliable. In my experience we cannot rely on another person to be consistent with feelings and opinions and the only way I can feel safe and rely on the people in my life is when I compassionately hold in my heart the reality of human nature. We all say or do the wrong thing sometimes! The sooner we get clear on this the sooner we can design the conception of our adventure around this fact and the less we will be affected by it.

It means we can love ourselves and all our loved ones more because we understand them honestly. No matter what happens we all have the power to forgive ourselves and others and move on. Let's be honest, when someone close to us does something wrong can we honestly say we haven't behaved in exactly the same way before? Invariably we have. Why? Because we are human!

If you have been witness to acutely painful circumstances in the past then by no means do I mean to make light of that here. I fully understand and respect that some things take a great deal more to process, whatever we are holding onto the path to forgiveness is incredibly healing.

We are talking more about trying our best not to hold grudges. When we have upset someone we can in fact take responsibility as soon as they bring it up, apologise, mean it and move on. We can either be right or we can be happy. Ask yourself does it *really* matter? Or are you more interested in getting on with your venture without the worry of having upset someone else on your mind?

Clear the mind, rather than giving the body reason to create unnecessary painful emotion. Be on good terms as far as far as possible with everyone.

When we need to tell someone they have done something wrong, practise it, put it in a praise burger and take responsibility for how it is making you feel. We praise them for something they have done well and then tell them what they need to address *in our judgment/opinion* and then give them more praise.

This is another tricky area to discuss, we are sensitive creatures and I do not mean to sound preachy here either. My intention with this section of the book is to simply flag up the detrimental effects it can have on our own path to feeling good and Finding Heart if we are complicating the relationships we have with other people in our lives.

Getting Good at Saying 'No'

Finding the best way we can to say no to people when we need to is important to Finding Heart. We can get the time we need without hurting those around us with statements such as this, "You know how much I love you and how much I love spending time with you, but I'm going to have a no people day tomorrow. It doesn't mean anything and when I am done we will go and do our favourite thing. Will you come and do that with me?"

When we ask ourselves, "How do I feel and what do I want" sometimes it means we have to be firm. If people come back to us a day later with a request or they want to change something tell them you will call them back. Then you prepare yourself and when you call them back you say the *exactly* the same thing again. "You know how much I love you and how much I love spending time with you. But I'm going to have a no people day tomorrow. It doesn't mean anything and when I am done we will go and do our favourite thing. Will you come and do that with me?"

Making the change to being authentic to our needs takes practise and when we get it wrong we simply take responsibility and apologise. Getting respectful of our own needs concerning others is all part of the Feel Good Game and learning to be aligned with our values.

It is OK to go things alone sometimes and when we get serious about making changes to accommodate our adventure we may need to spend more time away from people we love as we get things moving initially. Going back to our very natural need for love it is natural to worry that if we don't stay in close communication with all our friends all the time we may lose them and then we will be alone! Or perhaps we know the answer to this really. Great and true friends are always there no matter how much time has passed.

What is important is being truthful to our needs. Learning to resolve issues that arise with people does indeed take courage but we are Finding Heart adventurers now! Taking responsibility for something that may have caused upset is acknowledgment to ourselves we are doing our best, we are human and we are going to get it wrong sometimes.

Good friends know us better than we think usually and will be pleased we are up to something, trying something new or off somewhere new when the right time has come to tell them. When we are with them they have our attention and as long as they know everything is OK then all is well. Perhaps we are too quick to assume something is wrong if we are not regularly communicated with and told everything is OK by the other people in our lives.

Expressing Our Needs Constructively

It was pointed out to me once that all human interaction is either an expression of love or a request for love. Consider this as an idea next time you are with friends of family.

From our need to express or request love we are simply trying to communicate our needs when we speak to each other. Often we are not clear on what our needs are but when we communicate our needs in a loving way to our friends or loved ones they find it easier to understand our behaviour. Consider that when we see to our needs first it actually makes it easier to tend to the needs of others.

Conflict invariably stems from unmet needs. Behind our communications with each other are needs and the more quickly we can identify the need in the other person the better.

We are gentle loving creatures and we need love and understanding. The sooner we can understand our own unique way of expressing and getting our needs met the sooner we can be of more use to other people. We can learn to limit how often we communicate with people from a place of fear unless they are well chosen people who can support us.

Anger is just fear on its way out. Getting angry is part of being human and we repress anger at our peril because it will make us ill. I find it very helpful to remember that it is never what other people or the world says or does to us, it is *our* reaction to it. When we begin to experiment with the concept of taking responsibility for all our own feelings and reactions it means we take the blame away from someone else. When we blame other people for the way we feel and get very angry with them have you noticed the sad isolation we experience? No matter how long we delve into the illusion that someone else is responsible for the way we feel the further we descend into pain and anguish. There is no solution down there.

'If we wish to express anger fully, the first step is to divorce the other person from any responsibility for our anger'. Marshall Rosenburg

This fantastic quote from Marshall's work on non violent communication not only helps the other person but it also helps us. It helps to create a space where we can express our anger constructively and in a supportive environment. It's easy to talk calmly and sweetly about how to be angry and when we are experiencing it we just want to scream and cry. But if we can bring new ideas into our consideration and practise we will soon grow through our own experience. This is how we learn after all, when we do things ourselves we understand.

We must take the plunge and try new things if the way we are doing things is not working.

What we are trying to achieve here is a way for us to maintain a clear path in our lives so we can move forwards into our adventure. We do this one day at a time, instead of making New Year's Resolutions, make New Days Resolutions. Each day we move forwards, there is only the day today to do our best to keep the relationship with ourselves and others in loving understanding and forgiveness. We have work to do!

The Heart of the Matter

- ♥ We now take on the mantra *'How do I feel? What do I want?'* This is how we can cut through what is old reaction to circumstance and what is actually our truth.
- ♥ Avoid talking to or asking advice from people about a new idea in the early stages unless they have *direct experience* of working with what you are about to do.
- ♥ When we speak to someone who has personal experience of what we are dealing with they will give us advice we can use.
- ♥ If our adventure is based in the need for approval we must gently acknowledge that fact and consider again if what we are looking to achieve is definitely coming from our own hearts.
- ♥ Anything we are holding onto from the past may be blocking us from the possibilities of the future.
- ♥ No matter what happens we all have the power to forgive ourselves and others and move on.
- ♥ We can either be right or we can be happy!
- ♥ Finding the best way we can to say no to people when we need to is important to Finding Heart.
- ♥ When we need to tell someone they have done something wrong surround it with praise.
- ♥ Getting respectful of our own needs concerning others is all part of the Feel Good Game and learning to be aligned with our values.
- ♥ Conflict invariably stems from unmet needs.

- ♥ If we wish to express anger fully, the first step is to divorce the other person from any responsibility for our anger.
- ♥ When we see to our needs first it actually makes it easier to tend to the needs of others.
- ♥ What we are trying to achieve here is a way for us to maintain a clear path in our lives so we can move forwards into our adventure. We do this one day at a time.
- ♥ Take a moment to add any observations or resistance you are feeling into your notebook ☺

Our Adventure and Our Spouse or Partner

When we have been in a close relationship for some time and it is time to now focus back on our own progress then we must make this change carefully and considerately. Our spouse or partner tends to notice when we change our behaviour! Communicating this well by taking responsibility for our own needs doesn't have to be scary.When we are clear that our needs are now to commit to our adventure in whatever shape or form that is we must move on that commitment.

I was once contacted by a lady who invited me round to her house because she was in a very desperate place. She had got married when she was in her early twenties and was now still happily married with two children living in a great house and living a normal healthy life. But she was in turmoil because she felt that either she had to start attending to the calling she had in her or she was going to have to announce to her husband that she was leaving and moving out of the house.

So we searched together for the need in her that was clearly not being met. It turned out that for a long time she had needed to find her independence again enabling her to train in a particular field. She felt the opportunity to do this had been stripped from her due to being married so young. Whilst she loved her husband and her children dearly she had forgotten to love herself along the way.

The affect of this, left unchartered, was going to destroy her family. She needed to be heard and acknowledged, she had a person inside of her that had been mute for years and so I listened attentively for over an hour to this person inside. Once this person had permission to speak without the fear of judgement the needs emerged. In fact the needs were quite simple and I invited her to consider that she could attend to these needs and take the support and the love of her family along for the ride when she was ready to tell them. We set out clear achievable ways she could begin to re-establish her independence on a *daily* basis and most importantly how she could express these needs to her family in a way they would understand. This freed up the time and space inside of herself she needed to begin her training in the field she had chosen.

We are unique and bespoke creatures. We all have individual needs and we are all different. It is assumed that the same concept of marriage is going to work for everyone. That the same family values are going to work for everyone. From an early age we are impressed with fairy tales that show us how life and relationships are *supposed* to be. I can't thank the man enough for what he has given us but Walt Disney also has a lot to answer for! Rest his soul. At the end of each of his movies we could have had a little caveat that says. 'Hope you enjoyed the movie kids! It was created with love and the spirit of adventure. We would like to help you to realise it is just a movie and we are not suggesting this is how real life is or is going to be. In fact it is based on a 'Fairy Tale' which means it isn't really true and it didn't happen. It is just a great deal of fun and a creation for you to enjoy. Hooray! Let's get some ice cream.'

At the majority of the personal development seminars I have attended the trainers try to make sure that everyone has their partners present. Many of the people who choose to go these seminars are ready to take action. They have needs and they want to make a difference in their lives. When a person comes back from one of these weekend seminars they are walking on air. They have been made to feel so incredibly powerful and pro active.

If their partner isn't there too it will mean he or she is sitting at home all weekend worrying whether; they are being brain washed, whose credit card they have with them, the dent that might be in it and who will be coming back though that front door on Sunday evening. So the organisers and trainers invite you to bring your partner along. Otherwise when Sunday evening does come around and the newly charged highly motivated wife is sitting in front of her husband doing everything she can to get him on board and just as excited as she is about starting her new business when all he can feel is fear. Perhaps fear that he is no longer good enough for her, fear that his income is not enough to keep her happy, fear that he is losing his wife. There are a clear set of needs on both sides and what is likely to happen is an argument and confusion and a start to the new week with a big helping of unmet needs. SPLAT! There goes her little leaf of Cress.

Most people fear change, we all do and when a loved one appears to be changing beyond our understanding it is frightening. So we need to be clear of our needs on both sides and we must look to be super careful about how we communicate the changes we need to make to our partner or spouse. The problems can often arise because we have kept a need to adventure buried for a long while. Each time we get the urge and inspiration to begin writing that business plan we decide there is no point. 'It'll never happen' we say to ourselves and we continue to live our lives with the same routine which only produces the same results and circumstances. So when we suddenly reach boiling point and can't take the inaction any longer, we terrify our loved ones. It appears that it's very serious and its life and death if we don't *make this thing happen now!*

Consider this. A family are enjoying a lazy afternoon in the garden one Sunday. Two children Tom and Anna are playing contently. Thomas climbs down from a tree and notices a couple of planks of wood behind the garden shed. He thinks to himself he would love to make a tree house! He runs over and drags one of them over to the tree. Then he runs back and gets the ladder out the garage. 'What are you doing Tom?' enquires his Dad peering over the top of his newspaper.

'Going to make a tree house Dad!' Thomas announces with enthusiasm. His father smiles and considers going over to help him. Maybe once he's finished his Gin & Tonic.

Thomas is not only meeting his own needs but the natural and impulsive way in which it is sold to his Dad means he will probably get his help and support from someone who has the personal experience of building a tree house or something similar.

If we adopt a similar manner in which we can enrol our spouse then the change we want to make is coming from a place of joy and it is light-hearted. We will just be getting on with it and as it might mean a slight change in the routine of the week we will stay in close communication to ensure needs on both sides are met.

What if Tom had walked into the lounge one evening with a black cloud around him, switching off the television, sitting down and demanding that he and his parents had a chat instead? Then began to exclaim desperately that for weeks he has been wanting to build a tree house, it was all he could think about. He was angry his parents didn't give him the space to do it; he blamed them for his sleepless nights and if things didn't change real soon he was going to move into a tent in the garden. Tom probably wouldn't have done it like that; this is how grown-ups usually go about it!

Another lady I knew some years back had identified her need to start her own business and had carefully and thoughtfully enrolled her partner into allowing her the mental space to work on it. But she was complaining that she just did not have the time to get it moving. Early morning was not a creative time for her. So on going through her day carefully by writing down her routine over a weekly period she noticed that she watched a particular TV program at the same time every day. There was some resistance at first as you can imagine but soon she got into the routine of dedicating that time to her business and her partner respected that and her need at that point of the day. This lady went on to become financially independent by replacing her household income with the business just by using this time in the early stages.

What Others Might Think About Our Adventure

It was Helen Keller that said, "Life is a daring adventure or nothing at all". Helen was left deaf and blind at the age of 19 months following an illness. But she went on to write 12 books and was the first deaf and blind person to earn a Bachelor of Arts degree. Helen learned to communicate by spelling words into her hand. If Helen had gone to a particular loved one or friend of the family and informed them she was thinking about writing a book whilst accidently knocking a vase over there is every chance she would have been met with loving yet negative responses. Of course it would be so easy to say to Helen this was not meant for her. That it will only bring her disappointment and pain when she discovers it is just too difficult to do it.

This was clearly not going to stop Helen. You know why? It was because she knew her own heart. She knew what disability she had. She knew the risks but she went ahead in the knowledge this was the bespoke path for her. Imagine what she would have learned about herself and faced along the way. It must have been incredible. This is how we must think about ourselves; no-one can know our hearts and see our vision.

When we are in full flow and have committed to our adventure we are going to have to field the opinions of others in our lives. When I began my adventure in property investment which I used as an example for the mind map, one or two of the very close people in my life were convinced this was not a good idea. They told me I had good carpentry skills I had learned from my grandfather and if I was going to do something like this I would be better off as a carpenter living a simple life. I knew in my heart this was not what I wanted. I had tried being a carpenter and I all dreamt of was managing other carpenters and witnessing the transformation of a rundown property into a beautiful home. I wanted to be playing a bigger game. I needed an adventure.

The very first one I did *lost* me £18,000! But I could see where I went wrong and I not only learned a great deal about how to buy property but I learned a great deal about myself. If I'd had just gone home and listened to the advice I had received from my friends I would not have gone on to buy the second one which made the £18,000 I had lost back again and slightly more all within four months. I then knew that my heart was telling me to do things slightly differently because it was taking so long to find the renovation projects on the open market. So instead of using Estate Agents to find the next deal I discovered a way of finding properties myself using the internet. Again in the first year I only made a small profit. I had enough cash flow to live but somehow it wasn't working as well as I had anticipated. This was because the system I was using would only find me properties a long way away from where I lived. So this meant I had to pass these properties onto other investors who lived in those areas for a fee.

I had gained so much experience from running this system; how I worked in this field, what my skills were and what my weaknesses were. I knew it was time to take another step and move forwards again. So this time I began to network with other investors in my area. How were they finding their next properties? I soon discovered a way where I could get the attention of owners of property in my area and I teamed up with other investors. Soon we were buying a couple of properties a month and suddenly my dream came true. I was managing teams of carpenters and other tradesmen whilst seeing these run down properties turn into lovely homes again. I went on to renovate over 30 properties.

Finding strength and conviction in what we need to do and taking action according to our values will make other people's opinions fall into insignificance. This strength will build and build as we take action and see results. The way to avoid what others will think about an adventure once we are on our way is simply to just get out there and make it stronger and more stable. Soon the little plant will turn into a small tree and we then can giggle at other people bumping into it.

The reality of Taking up the Reigns

Feeling good and Finding Heart is the grounded energy that holds us firm. So we are not easily blown about by others opinions and distracted by them. Often they need us to stay where we are but this is not for their benefit and not for ours either. Some friends we love very much but the patterns can hold us to a particular lifestyle and the conversations we have are often the same. It is so easy to fall into a pattern of non action and losing belief in the self.

Finding the courage to take action is always bereft in uncertainty. We can never know what will happen, whether we will make fools of ourselves or whether we will do well. In fact the very term – 'You must take action' is nerve wracking to hear, especially when we are creating our own adventure, business or bespoke activity. It can feel like a blind action that may end in disaster from a certain frame of mind. Many concerns are raised such as, Will someone steal my idea? Will I be ridiculed or laughed at? Nature is cruel and people can be mean. But it is always those of us who do take the chance that move forwards. It is something that is part of the recipe of venture. The word adventure originally comes from the word *'auenture'* c1200 which means 'that which happens by chance, fortune or luck.' The meaning developed through "a trial of one's chances" and in c1300 "to risk the loss of".

This sounds a little worrying doesn't it? If we go out and take a chance will we end up coming back with less than we have already? Well this is the chance we take and we can never know. This is the great playing field of life. We can never know what is around the corner or even in the next minute. So the ability of Finding Heart is an essential basis to move from; we need this stability and belief. Simply feeling the sensation of our feet on the ground and dropping into our bodies, Finding Heart is not an aggressive state. It is not crashing forwards oblivious to our surroundings. Finding Heart is a strong place of love. It is a sensation of bright eyed alertness, of open and loving awareness; it is a union of heart and mind. A place where the mind is in service to the heart; the mind is still and ready; a yielding place where we are not easily blown off track; we are fed from the strength of our bodies and our intuition; there is no need for approval; there is no need to rescue others or take responsibility for others opinions. What is the word responsibility other than *'response-ability'*?

Life has always been an adventure from the very moment we were born. We are programmed with the courage to take new steps; literally. We have to go from seeing the world from our hands and knees to taking the chance of not only standing up on our feet but then leaning forwards and trusting our foot will come forwards and catch our weight. We do this with great loving encouragement from our parents or guardian, if we are fortunate. Then we begin to walk on our own accord and we fall down but something always makes us get up and try again. Then soon we are running and then soon we are riding a bicycle and even a skateboard or roller-blading. As children we have tremendous courage to try new things and go to new places. As we get older the stakes become higher. "To risk the loss of" becomes much more serious to us. Or does it? Or has the risk always been the same but the play area and toys just got bigger as we have?

Fear is often anxiety about being unhappy at some point in the future. So please remember the saying from the section on feeling good "Some of the worst things in my life never actually happened!" It is often a fear of fear that keeps us in our homes. That stops us making that call that has come up as a task on our mind map; that stops us enrolling on the course or stops us from booking the plane ticket. We are stopped by an imagination of events that *could* transpire if we were to take a step. It helps to think back to the past on this occasion when we have taken the chance and we have moved forwards, even as far back as learning to walk and ride a bicycle. We did come through that, perhaps with a few grazed knees and even a couple of broken bones but we made it and we are stronger because of it.

Life does hold us when we take chances and even when we spectacularly fail it still supports us and promotes growth and progression. There is *always* a way through something. Whatever it is, life does not stop when something goes wrong and humans have incredible powers of recovery. We do heal physically and emotionally.

"We all make mistakes, have struggles, and even regret things in our past. But you are not your mistakes, you are not your struggles, and you are here NOW with the power to shape your day and your future." Steve Maraboli

So how can we help ourselves to make use of this power if we have been living the same patterns in our lifestyle for so long? We keep coming up against the same routines and programmes in our minds that seem to stop anything new from happening. What can we do about it? Well one of my good friends is a therapist here in the UK and she is excellent at working with people who suffer with anxiety and cannot seem to move forwards with their lives as they would like to. When a new client comes to her and complains that their fear of leaving the house is getting worse and worse my friend will begin to break up the process of getting out of the front door into smaller bite size chunks.

So if for example the usual pattern for the client is to wake up in the morning and worry about leaving the house which results in him staying in bed for hours then my friend suggests getting out of bed and running a bath instead. Then if the usual pattern is to have breakfast in front of the television in his pyjamas the new routine will be to get dressed after the bath and have breakfast in the kitchen. After this the client is invited to clean their teeth and then put their shoes on. Then to find the house keys and his wallet and put them into his pocket then find his phone put that in his other pocket. Then the client is instructed to go and stand next to the front door.

What is happening here is that my friend is gradually changing the routine her client is used to and by doing so the thought patterns are changing. So instead of still lying in bed or sitting in front of the television having a lazy breakfast the client is now standing next to the front door fully dressed. This new course of events has stopped the usual thought process and programming from taking hold. Nine times out of ten what usually happens is once her clients actually try the new routine they find themselves opening the front door and stepping outside. This is because the new course of events has triggered new thoughts and possibilities which naturally lead to different outcomes. Most importantly it has illustrated that the imagination of the terrors lurking outside the house are simply that; imagination.

We can learn from this and in my experience this is an excellent way to begin to break the patterns we have in our lives that hinder us from taking the steps we would like to be taking towards our own adventures. We can begin to notice the same routines and decisions we are following week to week. When nothing seems to be happening it is time for us to change the routine and take small bite size actions towards the way we want to go. Even if it is simply introducing a new routine where we go for a walk after we get home from work, after that we eat and then we begin work on our mind map or business plan for an hour. Going for a walk breaks the usual pattern in our day. It could stop the thought pattern that leads us to snacking as soon as we get in that leads us to slumping in front of the television and deciding we are too tired from work to do anything. Making small changes initially almost tricks us into new thoughts, new courses of action and inevitably new habits.

The Heart of the Matter

- When we are clear that our needs are now to commit to our adventure in whatever shape or form that is we must move on that commitment.
- Finding strength and conviction in what we need to do and taking action according to our values will make other people's opinions fall into insignificance.
- Fear is often anxiety about being unhappy at some point in the future.
- Life does hold us when we take chances and even when we spectacularly fail it still supports us and promotes growth and progression.
- Whatever it is, life does not stop when something goes wrong and humans have incredible powers of recovery.
- When nothing seems to be happening it is time for us to change the routine and take small bite size actions towards the way we want to go.
- Making small changes initially almost tricks us into new thoughts, new courses of action and inevitably new habits.

What About When It All Goes Wrong?

If we indeed take our minds back to a time in our lives when a set of circumstances went wrong, or we tried something and it didn't work we will notice now that we were held through it and we are OK. It is the nature of life to support trial and error simply because the whole thing is evolving. It requires us to branch out and it has its way of looking after us. So instead we can choose to let go of this fear of fear and during our 40 day Feel Good Game we can experiment with actually dropping fear each time it arises. Furthermore there is always a positive side to most things. We could extend that to anything but for now every circumstance that seemingly went wrong has learning and something in it for us. So as we sit with the next step on our mind map that requires us to take action or try something new we can choose to take off the fear glasses we all tend to habitually wear, process any knots of feelings in our bodies using one of our techniques and say to ourselves: "Do you know what? I'm going to do it and feel great about it. If I need to try again until I get it right then that is exactly what I will do and I will *choose* to feel great about that aswell!"

I'm going to tell you a story now about a moment when I thought it had all gone so wrong I was not going to survive the night. Seeing as we have been working hard, here is a bit of entertainment for you before we go into the final section of the book; a chance for you to laugh with me or possibly at me a bit as we celebrate the uncertainty of life. Hopefully it will also help to illustrate how sometimes it is possible to come through even the most challenging of situations when we really do get it wrong along the paths of our adventure and still reap wonderful lessons as a result.

I was very lucky to spend a year in Africa during my time abroad and I travelled once into a very rural and beautiful part of Kenya, Africa with a friend of mine to go camping near a river. We had been in Africa for about 4 months and it was our last weekend together before my friend flew home. We could have gone anywhere to spend our last few days together but we decided to go there. We were so happy and sad at the same time, so proud of ourselves for successfully travelling over 6000km without any major problems or incidence and sad we were soon to be parting company. I was quite a seasoned traveller by that time with Africa being the last of all the continents that I had lived on and I was now quite experienced with keeping us safe through the countries we travelled through. But on this occasion I became complacent, we were emotional and I was taking for granted the risks involved with this sort of journey...

After we had set up camp, got the food on and settled down to enjoy our evening we both suddenly fell very ill. We became extremely dizzy and very sick. Neither of us were even able to stand in a very short period of time and began to vomit every few minutes for what felt like an eternity. I was literally unable to move very far let alone drive anywhere and it was only after a couple of hours I was physically able to pull myself up into our vehicle to find a homeopathic remedy I had for nausea. We had both contracted a dangerous strain of malaria earlier in the trip but had fortunately been treated in time before it became life threatening. We both assumed that this is what was happening, we were having a relapse and we were hours away from anywhere. It was one of the most frightening situations I had been in and I felt completely responsible for my friend. We were hopeless and entirely at the mercy of whatever illness had taken hold.

After several hours into the night the sickness began to subside and we were finally able to get into the roof top tent on top of our vehicle and out of danger from animals. I stayed awake all night to make sure my friend was OK as she slept. I just didn't know what was wrong with us and I couldn't run the risk of sleeping in case I never woke up again! This was how bad my fear had become in the loneliness and isolation of our situation. When morning came round we both felt better, the sickness had subsided but we both felt very weak. We knew that whatever it was had passed but we needed to leave in case we had another relapse. We were able to eat some breakfast to help restore our strength which we did over by the river a short distance away from the vehicle. Whilst we there a goat herder passed by us and stopped up on a small hill in front of us. He just stared at us for a few minutes and whilst we were distracted by him and his animals something bad was happening that we did not prepare for. When it was time to leave we had made a drastic mistake and one that I had religiously worked to avoid throughout the duration of our journey from Cape Town. We had left one of our money belts on the seat in the car and not put it back in the safe under the driver's seat.

This money belt contained all the cash we had on us and my friend's passport. It was gone. We think the goat herder had a second person with him and whilst he kept our attention the other was in the front of our vehicle. Our saving grace was that I had an emergency credit card in my money belt but so stupidly I had used our emergency fuel a few days before because we had reached Nairobi. We were dependent on the cash to buy fuel for the vehicle and we did not have enough fuel to get to a city where we would be able to use a credit card. So feeling horrendous from our illness the night before and with the fear that we may run out of fuel we began a very slow journey back to the closest town on the map. After an hour or so we ran out of fuel as we coasted into a small settlement. We were in a pretty vulnerable situation.

The settlement mainly consisted of a tent like shop with a corrugated iron roof set back a little way from the road. There was a similar construction next door that sold cooked food and drinks. Behind that there were some very basic single room dwellings with no-one to be seen. When we rolled down the hill towards it I had noticed a car which gave me a glimmer of hope there might be some fuel in it I could maybe siphon in exchange for something of value we had on board. This was about it as far as ideas went at this stage because I didn't fancy getting a lift in it anywhere as I couldn't leave my friend by herself with the vehicle and I couldn't take her and leave the vehicle by itself to be stolen.

I took a moment to gather myself so as not to appear desperate and got out of the vehicle into the dust and the searing heat with the worst hangover I had ever witnessed. I advised my friend to stay put whilst I investigated the situation. There was no one in the shop so I headed for the food shack and pulled back the canvas that hung across the door and peered inside. As my eyes adjusted to the darkness inside there was a wooden structure for serving at the back and some benches. There was a man leaning on the counter and another sitting down. They glanced up at me somewhat surprised having not heard a vehicle come in as a result of our truck dying half way down the hill.

"What does a man have to do to get a cold one around here?" I barked at the man leaning on the counter. And that was in fact the very last thing I would have chosen to say and I said nothing of the sort! I figured the best thing to do was politely sit down. My new plan was to strike up a conversation without appearing rude that I wasn't ordering anything because I didn't have any money to pay for it. Fortunately this didn't appear strange to my relief as they both seemed very pleased to see me. I told them I was passing through the area on my way to Nairobi and asked if they mind if I sat with them for a few minutes to get out of the heat. Again to my great relief they both seemed very happy with this and proceeded to ask me all sorts of questions about where I was from. It became clear to me quite quickly these two men were gentle souls and a foreigner appearing from the road was probably the most exciting thing that had happened all week.

I was aware that my friend was probably pressed against the window of the car staring at the canvas she had watched me disappear through, fearing the worst. So I excused myself and went out to the car to assure her all was well. I asked her to give me a little more time inside while I assessed our new friends and worked out a way to cleverly break it to them I was in fact in the market for fuel. When I turned around they were both beaming back at me with glee at the vehicle I had apparently turned up in. They slowly began to circle it as though it could fly and began to ask me another host of questions. I relaxed as the sensations in my body began to glimmer and I could sense my assessment of them was complete. It was time to enquire about the other vehicle I had seen and ask if they could introduce me to the owner.

"I am the owner!" one of them proudly announced. "Do you need some fuel?" he continued to beam at me as though this had happened every day. I considered for a second that he may even have been the goat herder but that was ridiculous, we had travelled too far by this point. I paused for a bit and then after making some involuntary and nervous squeaky noises admitted that we had in fact run out of fuel. But then I launched into the suggestion that if I could siphon the fuel from it I would make it worth their while but first I needed to see the vehicle. He explained that his car hadn't run in months and the fuel went from it ages ago, he was still beaming at me.

Before my heart had a chance to drop into my stomach he pointed behind me and said "But he has fuel!" There was another car approaching us and the two men danced excitedly across to it as it pulled up next to ours. Before I had a chance to do any assessments or make any new plans based on my feelings about the situation they knew the driver and had told him our situation. He refused to allow me to siphon any fuel from his car because he would then be stranded so he suggested he drove us into Nairobi if we paid him.

Being the only option of course we had to take him up on it. We covered everything as best we could inside our vehicle. Leaving it at the mercy of Africa was now our fate and taking bags with our cameras etc was all we could do. Both of the men had to come with us of course and we began the very long and animated journey to Nairobi. Having explained to the driver I only had a credit card we needed a garage that took Visa.

Everything turned out fine. I filled up our jerry can with fuel, my card worked and so we then drove to a cash point so I could pay the driver and we began the journey back to our vehicle. It was there and it was untouched. We were unbelievably grateful for the kindness of our new friends and lavished them with as much money as we could safely afford which in turn was their greatest need.

Regarding the illness, we discovered once we were back in Nairobi with our own vehicle that we had not in fact had a relapse of malaria or any other disease. You know when you get antibiotics from your doctor and they tell you not to drink alcohol with them? We had to take anti-malarial tables every day we were in Africa and the ones recommended to us back in the UK before we left were an antibiotic. When my friend and I arrived and began setting up camp as we had hundreds of times before we started out on the Gin and tonics. We had a little fridge on board for ice and it was all very civilised! This time around we were in very high spirits, literally. Reminiscing about our trip and so used to the outback in Africa we had finished a bottle of gin between us by the end of the evening.

We remembered we had not taken our anti-malarial tablet and so we both took one having consumed all that alcohol. I cannot describe the feeling to you even if I tried apart from perhaps being stuck on a fair ground ride for hours on end. Any movement whatsoever meant complete disorientation, a total inability to even sit up let alone stand and nausea like the world was ending. At the time I genuinely thought it was. I don't recommend it. I would like to mention the little homeopathic travellers remedy kit that had been bought for me as a gift. Something made me remember it during this episode and I will never forget the effort it took to get from the ground to opening the door of the truck to clawing my way into the passenger seat. To then adjusting my body enough to be able to get this little green box of magic out of my bag, it was a last resort but it was worth a try. If I had known what the cause of it was then it would have been slightly more bearable. But to witness my friend in the same state and being so far from any type of help; assuming we were in the final stages of a life threatening disease was definitely up there in my list of things going wrong during an adventure.

Inside the little green box was a list of all the remedies contained and what they were for. I found one that said "For constant nausea not relieved by vomiting". I held the tiny tube of little white tablets in my hand to search for any twitch of intuition I could sense in the depths of this ocean of sickness to tell if this was a good idea and going to help us. I went for it and waited to see what happened to me before I gave one to my friend. Within ten minutes the nausea subsided. It was after I gave one to my friend she finally fell asleep and I sat there waiting with the African night and my mind to see if it really was in fact our last.

Sometimes life throws us a curve ball and the situation I just shared with you was one I rigorously planned for to ensure would never happen to us when I was back in the UK looking at the map of Africa on my wall. All the preparation and thinking in the world cannot account for the mistakes we might make along the way. But wherever we go and whatever happens to us we can rest assured that in the moment we will know what to do even if at the time we are helpless in the middle of a desert. Even that situation in Africa makes me smile now when I look back at it. But had I let the fear of it happening to me back in the UK grind the adventure to a standstill I would never have grown and enjoyed the incredible experience I had travelling there.

There is no way we can be open, grounded and connected all the time. I do not want to suggest an unrealistic expectation that we are supposed to feel great no matter what happens and walk about like an enlightened warrior king or queen when we are given techniques, support and positivity. It takes time to create new habits that work to gradually dissolve the blocks that hold us back, but we can do it. No one I have ever met in all the personal development trainings and teachers I have met around the world have trained themselves to respond robotically in every given moment. But we can have be or do anything we want, if we can learn to believe in ourselves that we just need to take the next step in line with the feelings in our bodies and get out there and do it. We will get there one step at a time.

It is important to remember that we can limit how long we feel upset and anxious for especially letting go of the need to analyse and judge our reaction to a particular situation long after it has taken place. We *can* change our mood and this means letting go of our addiction to the base states of despair and hopelessness, which are indeed very addictive. Sometimes it is so inviting to announce the world as a bad place and hide, avoiding as much of life as possible.

From wherever we are we can always bring ourselves back to our hearts, back to getting in line with ourselves and where we want to go. Whatever it takes we can do it. When we are clear on what we value in any situation by asking what is most important to us right now we can simply return to our commitment to feeling good and get on with housing and nurturing our adventure. Let it go, feel good and move forwards.

The way back to feeling good in our hearts is *always* possible from wherever we are and simply choosing to take that next little step on our radar will keep us moving forwards.

So one we go now into the final part of the book...!

Daily Action

You'll notice that the people who tend to get things done are always doing something. My Aunt is a classic example, she bought up four children got a degree whilst doing it and also had a job at the same time. When I am with her she always seems to be walking around. I am often inspired by what she seems to get done. Living in a Jewish community she organises great big lunches and get-togethers. If something goes wrong or doesn't work out as she planned she just seems to walk about in a different direction until she finds a new way to do it. Actually doing something is important if we are to move forwards. The feeling we have in our hearts that is turning into a dream in our minds will be gradually processed through action. Taking action is what is going to see the feeling become a reality. But as we discussed at the very beginning this doesn't mean we are suddenly going to wake up tomorrow with our dream at our door step. Sometimes I think we wish this was the case that we could snap our fingers and our dream is our reality. But we wouldn't be ready for it, we need to go through all the emotions and hard work with our dream as a team together, working side by side until we materialise with where we want to be.

Get your HQ set up and feeling great and be clear and honest about how you like to work best. If you need to paint an entire wall as a blackboard the paint can be bought at any hardware store. Or if it's on a mirror you can buy pens that write on glass in any big stationary shop. If you find you are working hard on your adventure for three days and the fourth day you need to spend the entire day sleeping then give yourself what you need. It doesn't matter how other people do things, it doesn't matter what we had to do at school or university. This adventure is heart based, it's individual, unique and it's yours. It doesn't matter if what you would like to do has been done a million times before, this will be the first time it has been done by you. If no-one has done what you have done before and you need someone else on board don't expect them to have your vision. Be wary of partnerships, for two people to have identical needs and visions is very unlikely. Get the support you need but be really careful about taking someone on board because it simply feels scary to do it alone. Find people you can trust to get advice, you will find them. Get any contracts checked and double checked by an experienced third party. We are never expected to make big decisions immediately. Instead we can say, "Thank you, I will take some time to process this and I will come back to you."

Often with our own dreams and adventures there is no time frame to work to, especially if we are working at it alone. It can seem like a very lonely process when we are unable to share it with friends and family initially due to the risk of our idea being talked out of us but we can find all the reassurance we need inside of ourselves in these early stages by taking action. Appointing a key person in our life who can help keep us accountable with our progress can be invaluable if we need it. Remember that often the best action is simply to write down a question we don't know the answer to that is impeding us from moving forwards. Then from this we can design our next course of action and get out there and speak to people we need to.

We start to get passionate about our adventure and naturally create that impression when we speak to the right people. We become trustworthy and like to stick to our word. Once key people we need are involved we begin to create timeframes and commitments, the journey begins and we begin to see things take shape.

When we are Finding Heart and acting on it the world seems to fall into serendipity and it all boils down to one thing; commitment.

'But when I said that nothing had been done I erred in one important matter. We had definitely committed ourselves and were halfway out of our ruts. We had put down our passage money--booked a sailing to Bombay. This may sound too simple, but is great in consequence. Until one is committed, there is hesitancy, the chance to draw back, always ineffectiveness. Concerning all acts of initiative (and creation), there is one elementary truth the ignorance of which kills countless ideas and splendid plans: that the moment one definitely commits oneself, the providence moves too. A whole stream of events issues from the decision, raising in one's favour all manner of unforeseen incidents, meetings and material assistance, which no man could have dreamt would have come his way. I learned a deep respect for one of Goethe's couplets:

"Whatever you can do or dream you can, begin it. Boldness has genius, power and magic in it!'

W. H. Murray in *The Scottish Himalaya Expedition*, 1951.

This describes the magic of Finding Heart and it is also my experience. Life actually becomes easier once we make what seems to be the difficult decision. The easy path becomes hard but the hard path becomes easy.

Once we commit we know it doesn't matter if things take a new turn or we discover we need to make a change or do something different because we simply adjust and get on with it. Worrying about and trying to predict all this as potential problems when we still haven't committed is silly really isn't it? Like when we learned to drive a car, if we sat there and worried about the test for 6 weeks instead of committing to the lessons we would have spent the time anyway and not achieved anything. By the time we are ready for the test many days have passed but they have been days doing and moving forwards. Finding heart is in the doing, we can only experience the magic when we are actually in there doing it.

A Final Word

There will always be a reason not to do the very thing we would love to. We will find some sort of excuse. As long as we are comfortable and life is moving along relatively easily it is so easy to slip into doing the minimum. As long as the bills are being paid, the children are being fed and there is a holiday each year, why rock the boat? When we are reminded of the thing we would rather be doing by seeing an example of it or by bumping into to the person already doing it we make up all sorts of reasons to remain where we are.

If there are some things I can leave you with as you finish this book let them be these... Life moves very fast. Human beings have incredible powers of denial. We cannot get back the time we have spent. Is the potential pain and fear of taking action that we may feel now going to be worse than the pain of looking back as an old person wishing we had done something about the adventure in our heart? Don't give in to the 'easy alternative'. Don't give into the people around you who say you can't do it or you are fine where you are. You will know when you are living the passion and adventure in your heart. If you know you are not living the truth in your heart then remember no-one else on this planet will come and whisk you away and make it happen. Only you can do this. Begin it now.

We don't need to spend a fortune on personal development to try to heal what we think is wrong with us. Please, please, please don't wait until you are 'healed' as though it is a final destination with a certificate. If there was a magical cure out there that resolved all the parts of ourselves we believe are limiting us we would have found it by now. Who you are and where you are *right now* is exactly right to begin the adventure in your heart. If you are struggling with difficult feelings that overwhelm you then process them in the knowledge that they have their place in your adventure. It is when we have moved forward and gone out into the world knowing we aren't perfect with the courage to do it anyway that the magic begins to happen. Ask for the support you need along the way from well chosen people who have experience of what you are hoping to achieve, no-one of us have to go at it alone. Begin it now!

There is a book called The Hobbit by J.R.R Tolkien that has been made into a movie. It may not be your thing and if you haven't seen it or read the book it is about an adventure with a company of individuals who choose to embark on a journey to face a dragon and claim the riches it defends. The Hobbit known as Bilbo lives a pleasant life in a beautiful village but he is called upon to play a key part in this adventure. He refuses to be involved with it at first but he knows in his heart he must go. There is a scene when Bilbo is sitting in his chair in his lounge having just passed out after hearing what would happen to him if he got caught in the dragon's flame. He asks his wise friend Gandalf a question, 'Will I come back Gandalf if I come on this adventure with you?'

Gandalf replies, 'I cannot guarantee that and if you do, you will not be the same.'

It is through taking that step out of his front door that Bilbo begins a new journey of self discovery. He is wrought with fear and uncertainty. Convinced he is not cut out to go on any sort of adventure. But it is what is in *his* heart that will change the fortune of the company's fate. It is the flavour of who he is right *now* that he takes with him through that door. Along the way he finds the heart to do whatever needs to be done in the moment. The more he experiences that he is OK and that he can trust himself to do what needs to be done the more he grows and the more of his shadow and fear comes into the light. He will always walk with his weaknesses as does every other member of the company including Gandalf and the same goes for us. But it is through adventure we truly begin to know ourselves; not *change* ourselves, know ourselves. Walk your path. It is your right, your truth and your saving grace.

I believe in you. May you always find the light in your heart.

Getting in Contact:

If you need any help with the material in this book or if you would like to get in touch for any reason I would love to hear from you. Please send an email to:

willow@findingheart.co.uk

Recommended Reading

After you have been out there working on your adventure and you deserve a well earned break. In no particular order I highly recommend reading these books to help you with your journey into Finding Heart:

THE POWER OF NOW by Eckhart Tolle

(This is an excellent book written by one of the most influential spiritual teachers of our time. It is excellent to help us realise we are not our minds and the body is one of the keys to entering inner peace).

FEELING IS THE SECRET by Neville

(This short book is essential reading in my opinion. It suggests why it is so important to learn to maintain a good feeling environment in our bodies and the effects it has in helping us achieve our dreams).

THE CHIMP PARADOX by Prof Steve Peters

(I found this book incredibly helpful. It is a powerful mind management model that helps us understand how we develop particular voices and overwhelming feelings that seem to sabotage our success and what we can do about them).

THE ARTIST'S WAY by Julia Cameron

(If you have the slightest inclination that being creative in any sense of the word is an important part of you that might be squashed away for any reason, this book will be life changing for you)

Notes

Notes

Printed in Great Britain
by Amazon.co.uk, Ltd.,
Marston Gate.